A Culture of

An Inside Look at Los Angeles County's
Department of Children & Family Services

By
Julian J. Dominguez, LMFT
and
Melinda Murphy, M.A.

Edited by
Lee Barnathan

Strategic Book Publishing and Rights Co.

Strategic Book Publishing and Rights Co.
12620 FM 1960, Suite A4-507
Houston TX 77065
www.sbpra.com

ISBN: 978-1-62857-210-0

Table of Contents

Preface

This book is dedicated, with tremendous respect and admiration, to those Los Angeles County Department of Children and Family Services workers, past, present, and future, who have dedicated their professional lives, or a good portion of them, to one singular purpose: to protect children by responsibly empowering parents to rebuild and make their families whole again. DCFS has and always will have tremendous workers at all levels and in all job functions who care very deeply about helping families. These workers are unquestionably committed to bringing their skills, talents, training, creativity, education, and compassion to the families they serve.

These DCFS employees do an extraordinary job under incredibly challenging and complex circumstances and with limited resources, and they deserve profound ongoing recognition and appreciation for the service that they render to their communities.

The purpose of this book is to expose some of the most serious systemic deficiencies and defects that have impeded and/or prevented countless Children Social Workers (CSWs), Supervising CSWs, and other directly and indirectly supportive DCFS staff at varying levels from empowering their case families to help themselves. These pervasive and serious agency-wide dysfunctions have resulted and continue to result in corruption, mismanagement, coercion, bullying, and intimidation. Most importantly, tragically, and unconscionably, these problems have caused us (DCFS) to harm families.

DCFS staff has a very unique and complex set of challenges. Some are inherent in the work itself, as illuminated and partially explained by such constructs as vicarious traumatization (VT), which speak to the potentially devastating impact on the CSWs.

Other challenges stem from longstanding systemic deficiencies and defects.

By exposing these serious systemic problems, we hope to ignite an open, meaningful, honest, and inclusive dialogue free from all forms of retaliation. Those inside our DCFS culture, as well as key stakeholders from our communities, need to begin to talk about how we can come together and mobilize our strengths, passion, compassion, and unquestionable dedication to help families, address these systemic deficiencies and defects, and make permanent DCFS course corrections. We firmly and unequivocally believe that DCFS and its workers are driven by principles of integrity, honesty, and fairness, and are genuinely dedicated and committed to helping families.

We fully acknowledge the stress that our agency and profession are under as we discharge our responsibility to help protect children from abuse and neglect. We in no way make light of the pressures and scrutiny brought on when a tragedy occurs, such as when a child dies on our (DCFS) watch.

In no way do we mean to imply or state that DCFS has not, does not, or is not helping protect children from abuse and neglect. We also recognize our responsibility to give credit when DCFS has made great decisions and choices that have resulted in our families having profound and positive successes. We cite two very specific examples that represent the best of DCFS, when it has "talked the talk" and very clearly "walked the walk" in acting in the actual best interest of the families.

Our combined twenty-seven years at DCFS and the stories of hundreds of DCFS staff whom we have had the privilege of working with lead us to conclude that without such an open and inclusive dialogue committed to honest self-evaluation, appraisal, and course correction, our systemic deficiencies at DCFS will continue to handcuff our current and future workers from empowering our families and, unconscionably, harm an untold number of them.

A time comes when silence is betrayal.

—Martin Luther King, Jr.

It Happens More Often Than You'd Think

I was a supervisor-in-training when one of our receptionists came running to me, stating, "A grandmother on one of your cases is yelling in the lobby, 'Somebody had better get Hitler out here to get rid of all these niggers!'" I told the receptionist to have security escort the grandmother out.

That grandmother was Olivia Kramer (not her real name), a woman of sixty-six years and the caregiver of her two grandsons. I heard her leave our lobby indignantly, vowing to voice her complaints to the powers that be.

I asked the social worker assigned to that case to fill me in on why Olivia Kramer was granted caregiver status. I also asked to review the file. I learned that this was an Interstate Compact for the Placement of Children (ICPC) case involving parties who had relocated to California; the court in Arizona (state name has been changed), where they had come from, maintained jurisdiction.

The parties to the case were:
* Mother, age thirty-six, who resided with her father and thirty-year-old brother

* Mother's children, two boys, ages eight and six, who had been placed in the home of their paternal grandmother

* Olivia Kramer, the paternal grandmother

The state of Arizona had decided to place the children with this grandmother. I found Olivia Kramer to be not only racist but paranoid and under the erroneous belief that her grandsons had been sexually abused. She was hell-bent on telling everybody this. That included her fellow churchgoers, community members, and the children's doctor, therapist, and schoolteachers.

After observing one of her grandsons touching his genitals, she requested anal probes be done on the boys because she was certain masturbation was a result of being molested. A forensic sexual abuse interview concluded that the boys had not been sexually abused. But Olivia didn't believe the results. She aggressively accused the boys' maternal grandfather of having sexual intercourse with the boys. When that could not be supported, she accused the mother of having sexual intercourse with the boys. When that could not be supported, she accused the mother's ten-year-old daughter of having sexual intercourse with her little brothers.

The social worker disclosed to me that when she did home visits, she observed Olivia Kramer making the boys sit on the floor, as they were not allowed to sit on her furniture. She further observed that the youngest child appeared noticeably sluggish each time she went to see him and appeared to be overly medicated (Olivia had complained that the child was hyperactive).

The social worker also told me she didn't know why the boys couldn't go home to their mother. She further stated that Olivia Kramer appeared to be sabotaging her daughter-in-law's efforts to get her children back. Arizona had placed Kramer in charge of the mother's visitations. She didn't allow the mother to see the boys on their birthdays. She listened in on the mother's phone calls to her children and timed the telephone conversations. If the mother wanted to take her children for Thanksgiving, Olivia Kramer required all the mother's relatives to provide her with their social security numbers and personal data.

When the children returned to the paternal grandmother's house after seeing their mother, she would interrogate them. "Did your mother abuse you?" "Did she hurt you?" "Don't kiss your mother. She has diseases."

I called my counterpart in Arizona to speak to the supervisor on the case and tell her the myriad concerns we had about Olivia Kramer serving as the children's caregiver, and to ask why the boys couldn't be reunified with their mother.

"Where's the risk?" I asked. I pointed out that the mother had her three children from a previous marriage in her care, so it made no sense why she wasn't allowed to have these two.

The supervisor told me that the boys couldn't go home to their mother because she was "crazy." She clarified this for me. "She went on *The Oprah Winfrey Show.*" I learned that the mother had told her story of being a victim of domestic violence on the talk show. I told this supervisor that if the mother had gone on *Jerry Springer*, perhaps we'd have a problem. But Oprah? What's wrong with that?

Then the supervisor stated, "Well, the maternal uncle lives in the home and he's *that* way."

That way? I thought to myself. *What's that way?*

"Gay?" I asked.

"Yes," the supervisor said. "We can't have that."

I couldn't believe what I was hearing. I was being told that a mother couldn't have her children because a gay person lived in the home? Then the supervisor told me to watch my back with the grandmother.

I spoke again with the social worker. Her opinion was that this was nothing but a custody battle. Furthermore, the mother was doing well and should be reunified with her children. There were letters in the file from the mother's licensed therapist attesting to the mother's progress. The social worker reported that the boys appeared very bonded with their mother. Olivia Kramer was a problem and was not a suitable placement for the children. The social worker stated she had communicated this to the Arizona social worker to no avail. My social worker urged me to do something about the situation.

I called Olivia Kramer to voice my concerns about her behavior. While I was on the phone with her, I couldn't get a word in edgewise. She prattled on, "You know, she [the mother] had sexual relations with the boys."

I could hear the children in the background. I asked her, "Are the boys there with you?" She said yes. I instructed her to cease talking like that in front of them. She didn't stop, adding that the mother had always been promiscuous and had trapped her husband, Olivia's son, into marriage.

"SHUT UP!" I finally shouted at her. I had never before yelled at any person in my working life. But she kept talking without missing a beat, so I hung up on her.

The mother cried when I called her. She told me that her mother-in-law had always been able to manipulate social workers into doing what she wanted. She stated that the social worker in the other state had been helping her but then backed down after Olivia intervened.

"The social worker even lied in court," the mother said. "No one will help me. I want my children."

I consulted the boys' therapist, who said that Olivia Kramer said "incredulous things," appeared preoccupied with sex, and accused the mother nonstop of abusing the children. The therapist stated that the boys spoke fondly of their mother in therapy.

I put in another call to the supervisor in Arizona and presented my recommendation for the children to go home to their mother. The supervisor agreed to have the children instead placed with the maternal grandfather, who lived in the mother's home. The plan was to transition the children to the mother's custody after a certain time period had elapsed.

Because of Olivia Kramer's erratic behavior, a plan was devised to have the children visit their mother and then stay safely in the mother's home. I would then call Olivia to inform her of the court's decision based on DCFS recommendations.

The phone call to Olivia went as badly as I had expected. She expressed her disgust with me. She accused the mother and I of being "chummy" and "secret lovers." She said that she had hired a private investigator to gather information on the mother and that the private investigator was also spying on me.

Late that evening I received a call from the police, who told me they were at the mother's house. They reported that one Olivia Kramer was outside the home. She had called the police and told them that she was the legal guardian of the boys and that the mother wouldn't return them. I told the police the truth of the situation and stated that Olivia was not the legal guardian, only the former caregiver. The maternal grandfather was now the care-giver. I told him that the grandfather had placement paperwork that should be more current than Olivia's.

The officer said, "Between you and me, she [Olivia] is certifiably nuts." He went on to tell me there were suitcases loaded up in Olivia's car. The police suspected she was going to take the kids. "It's lucky for them you were able to straighten this all out," he said.

The next business day, I received a call from a Los Angeles ICPC supervisor stating she had received a call from Olivia Kramer. The supervisor told me she agreed with Olivia that I didn't follow proper procedure in re-placing the children and that "it needs to be approved by ICPC."

I explained what had transpired and asked her to call the supervisor in the other state to verify everything. Then I went about my business for the day. Later, I received another call from the ICPC supervisor informing me that the supervisor in the other state denied she had spoken to me about re-placing the children.

"What?" I exclaimed. I told her that couldn't be, and I repeated my conversations with her.

Then the ICPC supervisor said something that made my heart skip a beat. She spoke in a manner that made it seem like she was divulging a secret.

"I believe you," she said in a whisper. "Listen, you don't know Olivia Kramer. You don't know what she's capable of. She's going to have your job. You need to give the children back to her."

"What? No!" I responded. I told her I couldn't believe what was happening.

I made a flurry of phone calls. I called the supervisor in Arizona but only reached her voice mail. I called the attorneys in the other state to ask for help and explain the situation. The attorneys promised me they would bring the matter to the presiding judge's attention.

I updated my social worker on what was happening. She covered her eyes with her hands and started weeping. "They said they didn't speak to us? They're lying!" she cried.

I consulted my immediate supervisor, the Assistant Regional Administrator (ARA), and updated him on what was happening.

"Don't talk to any more attorneys on this case," he ordered me. "Something fishy is going on."

This was a Friday. The following Monday morning, the Arizona judge called me on my cell. He told me he was recusing himself from the case because talking to me constituted *ex parte* communication, but he wanted to know what was happening. I paused for a moment, remembering what my supervisor had told me. But then I thought to myself, *This is not an attorney. This is the judge, the fact-finding, impartial individual, and I can speak to him.*

I told him everything. He thanked me for talking with him and for my work on this case, and asked me to fax him my testimony. When it came time to fax my document, I realized I didn't have the judge's fax number, so I faxed the document to one of the attorney's offices.

A few days later, my supervisor called me into his office to tell me I needed to return the children to Olivia Kramer. He stated that complaints had been made and he didn't want to lose his job over this. He asked why I wrote in my testimony that the Arizona Child Protective Services was incompetent and corrupt.

I asked him to reconsider returning the children to Olivia. I told him that taking the children from the mother's home would be traumatic for them and that I feared the boys were going to be taken out of the country. According to the children, their grandmother "took little pictures" of them and put the pictures in "little blue books"—passports.

"She's going to take them," I emphasized to my supervisor.

"So, she takes them," he fired back.

I was dumbfounded. I exited the office.

Afterward, my supervisor told me he was taking me and the social worker off the case. I asked the social worker to fight this with me. She said she was sorry but she couldn't because she was the family breadwinner and couldn't risk losing her job.

I called the mother to tell her what was happening. She broke down. "You were the only one who was helping me," she said.

With a new social worker, Olivia made another allegation of sexual abuse, this time about the mother's ten-year-old daughter, who supposedly had sexual intercourse with the boys. The new CSW sustained the allegations.

Later, my supervisor and his supervisor (the regional administrator) demoted me because of insubordination in this case. By faxing an attorney I had disobeyed the order to not contact any attorneys, and I caused too many problems for the social workers in the other state. So, they demoted me to the job of regular social worker.

This decision caused a semi-riot in my office. My fellow supervisors were angry with my supervisor. They told me I did the right thing. The administration transferred me to a different office.

As I feared, the children were taken out of the country by their grandmother. Their mother calls me every Thanksgiving to thank me for sacrificing my job for her in doing the right thing.

Years later, while in court, I ran into the social worker who had taken over the case and sustained the sexual abuse allegations. She quickly came over to me, looked at me apologetically, and whispered, "That mother got her kids back, right? I hope so."

"No," I told her. "The children were kidnapped by their grandmother." I walked away from her before she could speak any further, because I felt nothing but contempt for her. I was sure she had toed the company line in sustaining the ridiculous allegations Olivia Kramer had made.

I received two phone calls from Olivia after she took the children. She sounded like she was threatening me. She told me she knew I had children of my own and that she knew where I worked. I tried to trace the phone number, but it was private.

The boys are now in the National Center for Missing & Exploited Children database. The FBI interviewed me and appeared to take the case seriously. But because the court had not given custody to the mother, there was nothing the FBI could do. Moreover, the foreign government was not cooperating.

The children remain out of the country to this day.

DCFS Social Work: A Primer

Social workers new to the Los Angeles County Department of Child and Family Services often erroneously believe that they will rescue children from mean and nasty parents, upon which time the children will look up at them with appreciation in their sparkling little eyes and state, "Thank you, social worker. You saved me."

Truth be told, those words most likely will never fall upon their ears. Rather, they might hear, "Fuck you! I'm not going anywhere with you!" from a teenaged youth just before he slams his bedroom door in their faces. Or they might hear, "Nooooooooo! Please don't take me away from my daddy!" from a sobbing small child.

Two major points these newbies need to know right off the bat:

1) Even if their parents harm them, children love them and want to stay with them. While there are always exceptions, this is a dynamic of child abuse that social-work professionals must understand.

When I was in training to be a DCFS supervisor (known as an SCSW, or Supervising Children's Social Worker), my trainer said that you can tell that a social worker's report has lies in it when you read, "Everything is fine in the foster home, according to the minor." A more accurate statement from the child would be, "Please write in your report I'd like to go home."

But every once in a while comes an exception. I remember a

nine-year-old girl and her six-year-old brother. Their mother routinely left them alone for days at a time while she used methamphetamine with her boyfriend at his house. The children were left to fend for themselves. They ate jelly from the jar with spoons. They went door to door asking their neighbors for food. When they were told it was time to go to a foster home, they took the social worker's hand without hesitation and never looked back. Sometimes, youths who have suffered severe enough neglect and/or have been berated by their parents too much don't press for reunification.

There are also those cases involving gay youths who come out to their parents or whose parents suspect they are not heterosexual, and the parents subsequently disapprove and treat them terribly.

2) The majority of the parents who come to the attention of DCFS are not horrible people. Yes, there are parents whose behavior toward their children is so egregious and heinous that they should never have had children. They total about 20 percent of the parents. The courts usually take care of this population, ensuring these people never get the chance to get their children back. But another 20 percent or so are completely innocent, or the situation doesn't merit having their kids taken away. The damage done to these families is unconscionable.

Pity the poor social worker who tries to correct the wrong and alert the court or a supervisor. Neither DCFS nor the attorneys who represent DCFS admits to making mistakes, so even if parents are innocent, DCFS's tendency is to make them appear guilty in some way, and that could include making things up if need be or blowing things out of proportion. DCFS does not have a mechanism for backing down. That same trainer who trained me to be an SCSW said in the very first session, "We should be ashamed of what we have done to some of the families we have sworn to serve."

What about the other 60 percent of the parents? They tend to have a myriad of issues, but some child experts propose that if a certain percentage of those parents received financial assistance, affordable health care, and the like, they never would have come to DCFS's attention. I can't disagree with that. DCFS needs to do a better job of identifying those families that shouldn't have DCFS in their lives. So, if this number constitutes another 20 percent, it's with approximately 40 percent of the parents that a social worker does some real social work in child welfare.

Common sense tells us that if a CSW has limited time to serve his or her case families, then a majority of that time should be focused on that 40 percent. If the CSW spends too much time away from that 40 percent, it increases the chance for circumstances to arise that could have been prevented had the CSW been there to sense or catch the problems.

These are the only cases that DCFS should focus on. The court usually takes care of the horrible parents: they are never given a chance to get their children back. That 20 percent shouldn't be in the system and shouldn't have DCFS in their lives. The same holds true for those families whose only crime is that they are poor with limited resources. DCFS could be of service to these families by keeping the family intact, connecting them with community resources, and employing strong social workers who respect the parents as individuals and who are doing the best they can with what resources they have.

Too often, I've seen social workers not joining with parents or trying to build rapport with them. They enter the family's home wagging their fingers and telling them what they should do. This approach doesn't work and only breeds contempt. It's poor practice and a recipe for failure.

I remember a social worker who went out of her way to alert an apartment manager that a mother and her seven children were not on the apartment lease (only the father was, and he had vacated the home due to domestic violence and substance abuse). The mother and the children were evicted from the apartment. The social worker had it out for the mother, whom she didn't like for whatever reason. The social worker was ill suited for this line of work.

Don't misunderstand: DCFS interventions succeed. I found that what worked was to treat the parents with respect. I knew I needed them to get better. Those who work in the system for an extended time learn that foster care is a disaster and doesn't work. The statistics are dismal for those youths who emancipate or "age out" of the system: According to a January 1997 Children's Advocacy Institute report, 65 percent emancipate without a place to live, less than 3 percent go to college, and 51 percent are unemployed. Emancipated females are four times more likely than the general population to receive public assistance. Furthermore, in any given year, foster children comprise less than 0.3 percent of the state's population, yet 40 percent of those living in homeless shelters are former foster children. A similarly disproportionate percentage of the nation's prison population is comprised of former foster youth. (For additional information, read "My So-Called Emancipation—From Foster Care to Homelessness" from Human Rights Watch. It says plenty in seventy pages.)

Throwing money at a broken system isn't the answer. Foster care providers do receive reimbursement for taking care of foster children, and licensed group homes receive on average between $7,000–$8,000 per month per child. That's like a parent spending $84,000–$96,000 per year on his or her own child. And with few exceptions, where the money goes each month is not transparent.

In all my years of social work with DCFS, I can count about five foster parents with whom I'd be comfortable leaving my own children. Many foster parents, I've found, did not love the foster children but took care of them like a business.

Another disturbing trend: child sex traffickers targeting foster children.

I would often tell the parents these facts, and I would implore them to fix the issues that led to their children's removal. I'd say to them, "I'm here to help you get your children back. You have all your parental rights intact. I will help you the best that I can, but you have to help, too. I cannot lie to the court. If you're doing all your programs, I'm going to make sure the court knows, and I will say great things about you. But if you're not doing your programs, I have to be honest with the court. These are your children. Nobody knows your children better than you. Your children need you to get better. You know deep in your heart that nobody is going to love your children like you do."

However . . .

If you work or have worked in "the system," you soon realize this sad, tragic, and horrific truth: This is a system in which countless confused, scared, or angry families come through our doors hoping to simply have their cases decided on the facts alone. These families hope to be treated with respect and dignity and have their cases be free of undue bias or prejudice. These families represent the majority of our families, and they are not seeking to have their wrong and often tragic choices or misjudgments excused.

The sad truth for far too many of these families is that they don't have much of a chance to receive justice or anything approximating it. These families soon discover that they have to compete with the unspoken yet ubiquitous edict that DCFS must protect the status quo, especially its bosses and its managers, at all costs. That means DCFS routinely and indifferently sacrifices the best interest of its case families. As a result, these families are left frustrated, discouraged, and hopeless. Many simply give up, leaving them damaged and scarred for generations.

These feelings of helplessness are not limited to the families. We social workers are forced to bear witness to the unfairness of it all, and in doing so become damaged ourselves. Even the countless courageous, integrity-driven DCFS staff members who, in trying to do what is in a family's best interest, attempt to expose the truth, either to their bosses or in a court report, soon find out that they never had a chance.

Many of us have left with amputated spirits after seeing countless families deprived of or delayed in the opportunity to reunify, reconnect, heal with their children, and be a family again.

DCFS has historically lacked the capacity to effectively self-assess and self-correct, even when its systemic flaws are forced into the light of day, and one would think that change has to come now because it's so undeniably clear and obvious.

There are rare exceptions. DCFS sometimes makes corrections, but these are usually forced upon it, often because of a lawsuit. In the settlement that came from the much-publicized case of *Katie A. v. Bonta*, DCFS was forced to concretely address and provide for the current and ongoing mental health needs of our dependent children.

There were (and are) untold numbers of families that could have been helped and empowered to heal, grow, and rebuild. But they couldn't because of the deeply entrenched, seriously flawed status quo that protects the broken system at all costs.

When one pries back the fingers of DCFS's tightly held grip on the status quo, one begins to see how its first contact and court involvement, removing children from the family over allegations of child abuse and/or neglect, is seriously stacked against the truth and the actual best interest of the family.

The petition that is crafted when children are first removed is pivotal in establishing the basis and direction of the case against the allegedly offending family members. An attorney that *never sees* or even has a single conversation with the accused family member writes the petition, and it usually follows the adage, "Throw enough mud at the wall and some of it will stick." This method is commonly known within DCFS, the logic being that *in court the allegations will be pleaded down to a lower level of severity, so we should stick it to the accused now because we may not get a second chance.*

Social workers, supervisors, attorneys, and other involved staff are not rewarded for their dedication and unflappable commitment to the facts that support the *actual* best interest of our families, the truth that is based on directly observable events that can be corroborated by confirmed credible sources. Instead, these good people are subtly and overtly rewarded, encouraged, praised, coerced, threatened, and even ordered to lie. That ensures that attorneys will use the harshest language possible in the petitions and/or court reports. Then the court accepts it as truth.

As I will discuss later in this book, phantom authors rewrite court reports. These phantom authors are supervisors, their bosses (ARAs), their bosses' bosses (Regional Administrators, or RAs), or even higher-ups. They remain in the shadows behind the curtain, routinely censoring, slanting, and omitting facts and sometimes even tampering with court reports, day in and day out. These are the very same court reports that can and do determine if a family is made whole again, if children will be returned to their mothers, fathers, or other family members.

What is most incredulous and disconcerting is that these secret ghostwriters, in the overwhelmingly vast majority of cases, never have even a single conversation with the family in question, nor will they take the time to just once say hello or say something ethical or responsible such as, "I know this is a very trying time for you and your children. I have authored some or all of your report and I chose the recommendations, so if you have any questions or concerns, please address them to me, not your social worker."

It would make the most sense, ethically and legally, for the report authors to be identified in court or to the families. Instead, these phantoms have absolute immunity from accountability for the decisions, judgments, and recommendations they write on the court reports.

Our social workers are subsequently left to pick up the pieces by being forced to sign court report after court report in which they substantively disagree with the phantom authors because they know the truth from their experience and training. These social workers are unequivocally told to sign, as to refuse would be insubordination, or worse.

A Family at Risk—From Us

Some time ago, after several months of working in a DCFS program that was being discontinued, I was assigned to work as a Children's Social Worker (CSW). The caseload I was given was in the "back end," meaning it pertained to Family Maintenance (FM) and Family Reunification (FR). FM involves children who are made dependents of the court but remain with the family; FR involves children who have been made dependents of the court and have been removed from their family. This was an FR case.

This case was known as the Sanchez case (a pseudonym to protect the family's confidentiality), and was considered a "high-profile case." This is what DCFS calls cases that have one or more of the following elements: a child death, a parent death, threats to a CSW, a family member who is a public figure, or a family member who has complained enough to attract the attention of the Los Angeles County Board of Supervisors or a very influential and powerful official.

Now, because of the serious life-or-death nature of these cases and/or because of the potential for increased scrutiny due to heightened publicity, high-profile cases are only given, in the vast majority of instances, to handpicked CSWs. These CSWs, generally speaking, have demonstrated strong writing and communication skills, strong people skills (i.e., they are culturally sensitive and tolerant and maintain good professional boundaries), and typically have substantial life experience. As they consistently demonstrate strong social-work knowledge and skills, these CSWs represent much of our most reliable, trusted, and seasoned CSW staff.

The Sanchez case involved a four-year-old child who had died. There were eight children in the family, all in the care of their paternal grandparents. The birth father had agreed to this in his living and care arrangement; the mother, by this point, had long since fled with the youngest child.

From what I read in the case file and was told by the CSW who had had this case before me, law enforcement had exhaustively investigated the death to determine if any criminal acts had been committed. According to records, after the investigation had determined that there had been no wrongdoing by any family member, all the children were "detained" (a DCFS word for "removed from their family") and placed in foster care six months after the death of the child.

After reading the records, speaking to the last CSW on the case and speaking with the family at length on several occasions, I don't understand to this day why the children were detained. Our legal system thoroughly and exhaustively investigated the death and did not find any criminal acts. In fact, our local ADA never opened a case. The detectives, at the insistence of DCFS, twice conducted interviews with all the children, the paternal grand-parents, and the birth father, and determined that the family had told the truth.

During the six months after the death of the child (hereafter referred to as the sibling), before the children were detained, the children were doing great, which the record reflected. While in the care of their paternal grandparents, the children had consistently attended school. They had had their medical and dental needs fulfilled. They stated that they were happy and doing well while also sharing sadness at the loss of their sibling. Two siblings were younger than the sibling who had died.

The autopsy report came back late, several months after the sibling's death. The report stated that the cause of death was "unknown/ undetermined." The report stated that the child had appeared malnourished and dehydrated and that there were ligature marks on the child's ankles.

The family told the investigators that the sibling had been sick for a few days, which could explain the malnourishment and dehydration. The family also stated that the children had been playing a game in which they would tie their ankles together. There was a popular animated film at the time in which children tied their ankles together as part of a game.

As I worked this case, one of my responsibilities was to monitor visits between the children and the father and paternal grandparents. The previous CSW on the case was relatively new to the field and around twenty-seven years old, and had run into problems with the father. The CSW told me that the father could be "a real hothead." Another CSW staff member who had assisted with the case told me that the father hated women and was a misogynist. The previous CSW also said that the father had gotten so angry and unreasonable during a visit with his kids that the CSW had to call his supervisor and ask the father to terminate his visit and leave the office.

As we discussed this case more, the previous CSW began to share his candid observations about the family, observing how bonded these children were with their father and grandparents and how consistently appropriate they all were. He said over and over that they really loved each other and he couldn't understand why DCFS had detained them.

At the time, the children had already been placed in several different foster homes and were constantly having problems with the foster parents. It became very clear, very fast, that the vast majority of the issues that the children were having were simply because they were angry and scared from having been taken away from their family. The children were also extremely confused. They couldn't understand why they had been taken away. From their point of view and personal experience, their father and paternal grandparents had always taken very good care of them and had always met all their needs. They had always felt loved. Now, they were separated and had very little contact with each other.

As a result, the children started developing clinical-grade symptoms such as depressed mood, markedly diminished interest or pleasure in almost all activities, insomnia, recurrent and distressing dreams, intrusive thoughts and images, fatigue or loss of energy, feelings of worthlessness, outbursts of rage, diminished ability to think or concentrate, hyper vigilance, avoidance behaviors, feeling of detachment, acting or feeling as if the traumatic event were recurring and crying spells.

What was even more inexplicable was that the one-year-old boy was placed in what is called a "pre-adoptive home" some sixty miles from where the father and grandparents lived. This was a Family Reunification case. That meant the father, the only parent who was an active party to the case, was court-ordered to have reunification services. This meant that DCFS should not have been making any efforts to adopt any of the children. Yet the youngest child was sixty miles away in a pre-adoptive home. Why?

Furthermore, the CSW adoptive worker assigned when the department placed the one-year-old child in the pre-adoptive home told the young couple hoping to adopt the child that the father would never get his kids back, especially because he continued to live with his parents. This young couple was being set up for a very hard and crushing fall, which was too bad because our adoption worker and agency supervisor should have known that even though the father still lived with his parents, had some anger issues, and had a child that died mysteriously, he still had his parental rights.

As if it wasn't already bad enough, one of the older siblings, a twelve-year-old girl, was then placed in the same pre-adoptive home. When she realized that the couple wanted to adopt her brother, she became anxiety-ridden and perhaps even somewhat uncooperative as it gradually occurred to her that her family was at risk of being permanently torn apart.

This twelve-year-old was constantly in conflict with this young couple because she had heard the couple make statements to her younger brother about how he was going to be a part of their family. She also heard them repeatedly make disparaging remarks about her father and grandparents, whom she loved and missed terribly.

In the meantime, this older sister, not knowing how to handle the situation but feeling compelled to do something, anything, to prevent her brother from being ripped away forever by this invading young couple, began to exhibit what are known as "parentified" symptoms and reactions. "Parentified" is a term that is usually associated with children who have been inappropriately shouldered with the responsibility of taking care of their younger siblings; that is, children who become pseudo-parents. On one occasion, this older sister took her younger brother into the bathroom and locked the door. The younger couple saw this as the older sibling trying to hurt her younger brother and putting him at risk. They built a case that the older sibling was unstable and that they needed her placed elsewhere. She was.

The young couple eventually found out that they would not be able to adopt the child. Up to that point, they were building their lives around what they believed would be a sure adoption. Over the several months that this one-year-old was in their home, this young couple had developed a very strong parental attachment and felt that the child was now theirs.

As this couple began to realize that the child they had counted on adopting might be taken from them, they became more desperately hopeful that the father ultimately would be denied his parental rights. Whenever all the kids visited their father and paternal grandparents, this young couple would fabricate story after story of how this one-year-old was being mistreated. They would say that he was being fed wrong, and that he was being fed improper foods. They stated that they had to rush the one-year-old to the hospital over and over because of what the father was feeding him during the visits. They also claimed that the father and the siblings ignored the one-year-old and did not provide adequate supervision for him. They also made a host of other baseless allegations of mistreatment. After every visit came a nonstop series of complaints, which almost always included this young couple allegedly having to rush the child to the hospital because he vomited. This did not surprise me because CSWs often encounter this type of behavior when one side of the family feuds with the other side in an ugly custody battle.

This young couple, whom I watched for several months, slowly came to the painful realization that what they had been told much earlier by their own agency and by CSWs was not the truth and never was, that they were simply a placement, and that this child, whom they had held out to family, friends, and community as theirs, wasn't theirs and never would be. As this couple began to slowly and painfully start to accept this fact, I watched them go through all the stages of grief and loss. They were crushed, angry, confused, and emotionally and psychologically devastated. Their loss was profound and so unnecessary.

Why was this young couple led to believe that this child was a sure adoption, despite the fact that the father had a Family Reunification case with all his children? Why was this couple so misled that they didn't know the father was fully compliant with every court order, maintained consistent contact with all his children, and most importantly had never placed any of his children at risk for abuse or neglect?

Just as damaging, if not more so, was the continued detainment of the other children. Many had problems related to foster parents mistreating them. There were reports of foster parents locking the children out of the house, and a report that one child was pushed onto the floor and held down by the foot of her foster parent as the foster parent made disparaging remarks about the child's father and grand-parents.

Some of the other Sanchez children were also becoming parentified to some degree. These children, like their twelve-year-old sister, were becoming anxiously protective of their younger siblings. These children unfortunately were exhibiting distress when talking about their siblings, stating how they couldn't stop thinking and worrying about their siblings and were having a hard time sleeping because of their constant worrying. These children also talked about not being able to concentrate in school.

After the twelve-year-old sister was moved from the home of the young couple hoping to adopt her brother, she was placed with her three sisters. She was ecstatic, to say the least, to be with her sisters but still carried the weight and burden of worrying about her baby brother. As it became apparent that the one-year-old should never have been placed in a pre-adoptive home, I began to make what would be several attempts to have him moved. However, despite all the evidence of previous errors and all the evidence that many people's lives were being genuinely, even irreparably, hurt by DCFS mistakes, my office administration continued to block all efforts at reunification in this case. Why? I never reached a clear answer to this question, but to me it was blatantly obvious that my office administrator wasn't willing to take any concrete or effective steps at genuine reunification no matter how appropriate, warranted, and critical reunification was for this family.

With the exception of my reports and my attempts to expose the truth regarding this family essentially being held captive by DCFS, anyone who took any interest in this case, including the court, was given a constant diet of false information about how this father and his parents were a danger. DCFS was bound and determined to keep this case and family frozen in place.

In our DCFS culture, we have unwritten laws of "just in case" and "not on my watch." When it comes to making the decision to begin working toward returning children to their family, most of the decision making usually comes down to the regional administrator, although a supervisor and an assistant regional administrator are often also involved. If this group of people feels that it's just not worth returning children to their families because they personally speculate that some of the circumstances in the case make it "too risky," then they send out a clear statement or signals to prevent it. This fear of possibly making a decision that may come back to hurt them or that might somehow disrupt their current standing, possible future promotions, bonuses, and retirement sometimes causes them to be too cautious or even apathetic in reunification efforts. It is the families, the parents, and the children who then suffer.

This case is a classic example of systemic dysfunction in action. What's more, this power is absolutely devoid of any meaningful checks and balances. Our department's position, code for an RA or maybe an ARA and/or supervisor decision, demanded that the Sanchez kids be prevented from ever reuniting with their father or paternal grandparents. So the department made certain to slant and even blatantly alter every report on the Sanchez family sent to court. The department was absolutely intent on giving the impression that the father and his parents were not appropriate caregivers, were uncooperative with the department, and even acted in ways that would risk child abuse or neglect if returned. Their "position" was a complete lie.

Of course, our department ran into a huge problem when I started submitting my reports, which ran completely contrary to the department's position. When I reported to the court what I was seeing and hearing regarding the family, specifically about the father and the paternal grandparents, the court began to ask the obvious question, "What's really going on?" I was the first person to share information that described the father and the paternal grandparents in a positive way. This got me in some serious trouble with my ARA, who made it very clear that I was supposed to follow suit with the "at-risk" position regarding the family that the department had taken. In fact, my ARA deleted facts from my court report and submitted it without any DCFS signatures because it ran contrary to the department's position.

At this point my ARA called me into a meeting, and we were joined by my supervisor, a real good guy with tremendous integrity and guts who always stood up to our administration in support of our families and his CSWs. In this meeting, my ARA read and told me in no uncertain terms what impression I was supposed to have and what position I was supposed to take regarding the Sanchez father, his parents, and this family. The majority of the meeting consisted of this person telling me— instead of asking me—what I was seeing and hearing regarding the family.

The meeting ended abruptly, however, when I said, "That's not my experience with this family." I'll never forget what my ARA said as the meeting closed: "I used to be like you. I used to be a fighter, but then I decided that I can choose to work here or not. I choose to work here." The insidious message and thinly veiled threat were perfectly clear.

DCFS is such an enormous bureaucratic organization spread out over such a wide geographical area that each individual office functions as its own fiefdom. The office organizational structure is designed so that the RA holds all the power. Subordinate managers and supervisors are mere appendages of the RA. In many cases, the RA demands blind loyalty and absolute obedience.

Each RA has two to three ARAs. Dissension of any kind among the ARAs is not tolerated and is dealt with quickly and harshly if it occurs. ARAs have supervisors working under them, and it's understood that these supervisors are only hired by ARAs on the unwavering condition that they offer blind allegiance to the ARAs, who have already pledged absolute, unquestioning loyalty to their superior, the RA.

This inflexible, fear-motivated, power-grabbing hierarchy that can manifest itself at will within the DCFS system severely affected the Sanchez case. The family would see their children removed and returned three times in approximately five years. With each and every removal, the department used its considerable unchecked power to justify ripping these children away from their father and paternal grandparents. Their family was seriously, clinically traumatized many times over. Without question, the Sanchez family will forever be indelibly scarred. DCFS knowingly, consciously, and with premeditation placed this family at risk.

We did this.

A Professional Identity Crisis

The job of a Children's Social Worker is arguably one of the most important, complex, and challenging jobs in our communities. However, we have seen disturbing evidence that the Department of Children and Family Services is facing a severe identity crisis. Helping protect children from future abuse and/or neglect by supporting their families as they work on addressing their "at-risk" issues is critically important. This is why we maintain that such a crisis within the DCFS is an immediate and serious problem that deserves open and honest discussion.

The nature of this identity crisis that affects DCFS from top to bottom could be demonstrated in part by taking a survey and asking any combination of ten CSWs, administrators, and supervisors the following three questions:

1) In relation to your experience, what is a social worker?

2) In relation to your experience, what is the job of a social worker?

3) In relation to your experience and personal observations, what are the actual priorities of a social worker?

The answers might look something like this:

1) A person who is tasked with the responsibility to maintain a caseload of children and their families.

2) To assist and monitor the court orders and compliance of their case families.

3) To report back to the court what families have or haven't done regarding the standing court orders.

Additionally, the voluminous DCFS policy book that CSWs read when they're in training and on the job, as well as the materials that they receive from mandatory and non-mandatory future trainings, will emphatically and unambiguously state that CSWs must always act in the actual "best interest" of their case children and families.

However, if CSWs could speak frankly without fear of retribution, many of these well-meaning workers who should place the welfare of their case children and/or families above all else do not feel able to do so. If they felt free to speak the truth, they would say that they are being made to do whatever they're told without question or hesitation, and if they do otherwise, they would find themselves under threat of discipline. They are fully aware that to resist certain morally questionable directives may mean putting any hopes of advancement or even their entire careers in jeopardy. They realize that in demonstrating reluctance to go along with these directives, they may even run the risk of facing trumped-up charges on grounds of insubordination.

Many of the true responses would sound like these actual quotes from many past and current conscientious, hardworking, and deeply caring CSWs, supervisors, and ARAs:

"My job is to make my boss look good."

"My job is to protect my staff [CSWs] from my administration and the department."

"My job is to do whatever I'm told, regardless of whatever it is, so I can keep my job. I was counseled once, warned, by my former supervisor that I always seemed upset, so now, no matter what, I smile, always smile, so he can't write me up."

"It doesn't matter what the job of a social worker is here, they don't care about families, just themselves. One supervisor summarized it perfectly with an acronym: FUCMA, which means Fuck You and Cover My Ass."

"After working here, I don't know what a social worker is. It doesn't involve social work, though."

"I wish I could do social work, but I've pretty much given up. I earn a check and pay my bills and pray I can tolerate this place until I retire."

"They don't care about families, they just care how they look at the end of the day. They're much more concerned about looking good instead of doing good, or doing the right thing."

CSWs often find themselves confused, frustrated, and silently resentful and angry. They were told when they were hired that they were going to have an opportunity to do actual social work. They were told that they were going to be able to prioritize and act in the actual best interest of families and that they were going to make a difference by using their skills, education, training, and inherent compassion and empathy.

Instead of finding opportunities to serve, CSWs suffer because they feel misled and, to some extent, betrayed. They feel that they were basically sold a bill of goods, that they were victims of a carefully orchestrated bait and switch.

The inevitable and tragic reality, given the culture of fear and intimidation at DCFS, is that CSWs are left in a constant existential struggle for meaning and purpose. CSWs find themselves forced to continually reexamine just who and what a CSW is. They are faced with sadness and sometimes anger over what they are forced to do and say, over and over and over, lying in a report as the ever-present threat of "or else" violently crashes against their own morals and ethics. Thus, they find themselves in an emotionally fatiguing, spiritually crushing identity crisis that continues perpetually.

The CSW most acutely experiences this is in writing court reports. These reports, whether they are the typical six-month review known as a Status Review Report or an interim report called a Progress Report, have two primary purposes.

First, these reports are supposed to represent the worker's evaluation of his or her case family's status, including how well the family is complying with standing court orders. Typical examples would be whether the father or mother is attending court-mandated drug counseling sessions or going to their court-ordered parenting classes.

This evaluation is also intended to provide an opportunity for the CSW to tell the court how the family is progressing with its case plan. A case plan is a plan created by the CSW and the family that establishes a set of expectations for the family to meet, including the court orders, so that the parent(s) can eventually reunify with their child(ren).

It's important to note that these evaluations are based on the CSW's *direct observations* as well as the direct observations of other helping professionals, community partners, and service providers such as teachers, therapists, doctors, and social workers from other community-based support agencies.

The second and equally important purpose of the court report is for the CSW to make a recommendation based on his or her evaluation. The CSW will, in many cases, include supportive and collaborative documentation on what he or she has personally experienced while observing the family interact, and solicit verbal and written reports and statements made by other community partners and service providers also working with the family.

The tragic truth for far too many CSWs is that quite often they are forced to write court reports with evaluations and recommendations that do not reflect what they have directly observed or what they have personally experienced with the families. These CSWs quite often are forced to omit what they know to be the truth about the families based on their direct contact and work with the families. CSWs, time and time again, are told that they have to omit or change what they have directly observed or personally experienced simply because it is inconsistent with a position taken by their supervisor, ARA, or RA.

Throughout the Los Angeles County DCFS, CSWs are constantly forced into this bind with no other option. In some cases, these CSWs have sympathetic supervisors who also feel powerless to simply report the truth to the court. They are repeatedly forced into a personally crippling moral crisis.

CSWs believe that if they refuse to write a court report that they absolutely believe is false or substantively inaccurate, biased against the family, or harmful or potentially harmful to the family's well-being, they will be labeled as "uncooperative," "not a team player," "soft on abuse," "siding with the parent," "doesn't represent the department very well," or, worst of all, "insubordinate." CSWs and many DCFS staff perceive the "insubordinate" tag as a vocational kiss of death. The supervisors and administrators who create and circulate these labels are the very same individuals who force the CSWs into the crisis to begin with.

CSWs are forced into an unconscionable and unthinkable choice: "Do I tell the truth and refuse to lie or do I simply go along, again, and keep my job? After all, my own family has to eat, right?"

Supervisor after supervisor and administrator after administrator will tell a CSW over and over to work with a family by doing the following: "Do your best to help them," "Fight and advocate for your family," "Sympathize and support your family," "Be firm, honest, and straightforward, but be fair and reasonable and patient with your family."

But then, the CSW is denied the ability to tell the truth in the court report as to what he or she observed and experienced, which is often corroborated by documentation of other service providers. This practice is emotionally and spiritually crippling and can be psychologically damaging.

Far too many CSWs have to work and live in a state of fear and personal crisis. CSWs try to somehow balance this, but it still takes its toll. CSWs find themselves experiencing a variety of devastating depressive symptoms such as emotional fatigue, irritability, hopelessness, crying jags, sleep disturbance, diminished self-esteem, difficulty concentrating, anger, resentment, growing relationship conflicts, loss of emotional and physical intimacy, isolation, avoidance behaviors, diminished capacity for empathy, substance abuse, and on and on.

It's very possible, as it has happened countless times and continues to happen, for a court report to be so altered from the actual facts and truth that the only true parts are the names and relationships of the parent(s) and child(ren) and nothing more.

A supervisor or administrator can decide, based on a variety of factors such as prior court reports; personal feelings, biases, and beliefs about the parent(s) and/or child(ren); lack of cultural sensitivity and knowledge; and *their personal liability to exposure* to take a position that is substantively at odds with the facts regarding the CSWs case family. This fact-less or fact-poor position then becomes the only acceptable standard to use when writing a court report.

What is perhaps most disturbing and tragic about this long-standing practice is twofold: CSWs are forced to legally represent themselves as the author, and the supervisor or administrator, in the vast majority of cases, has *never met or will never meet* the family in question.

Equally troubling and tragic is that this same supervisor or administrator has often unilaterally and without any CSW consultation decided to dismiss the CSW's direct observations, training, insight, professional gut instinct borne of years of experience, and, in most cases, countless hours of face-to-face contact with the family. The result substantially or completely marginalizes the CSW, as if she or he wasn't even involved.

In these all-too-real and far-too-frequent instances, these ghost authors never have to take any personal responsibility or be held accountable for their actions and decisions. Our DCFS court report practice enables these ghost authors to say anything, write anything, order and compel CSWs to write anything they decide should be written, or omit anything they feel should be omitted. Then they don't have to sign the report, so they're not the actual authors in the court's eyes and don't have to hold themselves responsible or accountable. Instead, the CSW is forced to legally take the full weight of responsibility for the report. These CSWs even have to enter court and swear that their report represents the facts and "the whole truth and nothing but the truth."

There are also many, many good supervisors and administrators with unquestionable integrity who deeply care about the families under their charge, care about their CSW staff, and also find themselves in the same crippling identity crises.

Once on the job, it becomes very clear very quickly to CSWs that they aren't vital community partners that *only* act in the *actual* best interest of their case families. CSWs, having to struggle with the inevitably huge toll of coming to terms with what and who exactly they are, can understandably become saddened and apathetic about the reality that they may not have much opportunity to genuinely make the kind of positive difference in the lives of their case families that they had hoped to and that they had worked so hard in their studies and training to do.

These CSWs find themselves experiencing a slow death of spirit, of the will to do the right thing, after they or their fellow CSWs try to tell the truth and advocate for the family, and then experience the punishing reality that results.

Once resigned, CSWs are left guessing, frustrated, and puzzled. CSWs aren't sure if they're supposed to be an extension of law enforcement, i.e., a plainclothes cop, protecting "us" against "them," or if perhaps they are meant to be an undercover agent or spy, trying to find as much dirt as possible on the parents named in the petition's allegations.

Or maybe they think they're prosecutors, always gathering data that will later be used to win the case and defeat and crush the opposition at all costs, the opposition here being the attorneys representing the parents and children in court. Or maybe still, they find that the job of a CSW resembles that of a defense attorney trying to protect his or her clients from the win-at-all-costs, morally bankrupt department and some, seemingly morally indifferent counsel for Los Angeles County.

So when CSWs try to understand and define their identities—what exactly a social worker really is, what their job actually is, who they feel forced to become professionally or who they feel they're becoming, and what their priorities really are—it becomes an almost impossible dilemma.

They find themselves mired in an identity crisis that runs deeper than knowing how to define one's professional identity. It is also a crisis anchored in the reality of not being allowed to be who they were hired to be: a trained, caring, educated, helping community partner who desperately wants to help.

A Confession

I live with the same tremendous guilt that so many of my fellow social workers desperately try to manage day in and day out. This guilt results from writing false statements in court reports, omitting facts, and making claims about families that aren't true or right, but simply and unequivocally wrong.

I've made statements to children and parents with whom I was assigned to work that I knew were lies, and that would create more distress in their already tumultuous, fear-ridden lives. I've made statements that I knew were going to run the very real risk of destroying what little hope they so desperately clung to.

When many families first come to DCFS, they repeat the following mantra: *Maybe things can still turn around, and maybe my family can still be made whole again. Maybe these folks really care and won't judge me and condemn me for my "screw-ups." Maybe they'll be able to see past that and will help my family and I become whole again.*

As a DCFS employee, I live in a spiritually punishing, morally crushing environment in which I constantly wrestle with feelings of shame. Oftentimes, I feel powerless to do what I know to be the right thing. I've witnessed too many of my colleagues suffer as they desperately try to come to terms with what they have done or have failed to do.

I've heard countless social workers, including myself, make the following statements: "I feel so horrible for my family. I didn't want to say those things, but what choice did I have? I need to feed my family, too." "I didn't want to say that when I was on the witness stand, but I was ordered to." One social worker lamented with obvious pain and deep regret in her expression and voice, "I told the court that the mother didn't have a bonded relationship with her child, but she did, she really did. Oh my God, what have I done?" That mother, as a result of this social worker's statements on the witness stand, lost her parental rights.

We avoid self-reflection and introspection at all costs because we know that we will be unearthing tortured memories of the times we failed to stand up and speak the truth, or failed to do so as often as we wanted to. In these painful and crippling moments, which are often characterized by self-loathing, we remember how we failed to summon up enough courage to stand and refuse to be silenced. We failed because of a paralyzing fear of going against our agency's administration. Our deeper fear is that we won't be able to feed and clothe and provide for our own. "I'm just following orders, right? What choice do I have?"

I live with the guilt of testifying in court or simply being present as a DCFS "representative" and never uttering or hinting at the truth, the truth being what I saw with my own eyes and heard with my own ears. I've felt so afraid that if I even whispered small shards of the truth of what I've observed and personally experienced with my assigned family, the administration would quickly and unsympathetically retaliate against me. This has left me feeling utterly powerless to do what I know to be in the best interest of the families I have been charged to help.

We're constantly told and reminded, "You're representing the agency, so you need to write, or not write, and say what I'm telling you, or what I'm being ordered to tell you . . . or else." Those last two words carry so much power and become the amoral, uncaring, and ubiquitous force that lurks around every corner of our workspaces and realities. We come to work knowing that "or else" is always watching, listening, and ready to attack at any sign of dissent.

We tell ourselves, "I'm good at what I do and I work my ass off to help my families, so they won't get rid of me." However, years of dedicated service and heartfelt concern for families, as well as a strong and consistent work ethic and professional work quality, are no protection against retaliation. Those who dare to cross the line and speak the truth or stand up in service of the actual, genuine best interest of families are shown no quarter by the administration. This characterizes our culture of fear and intimidation.

Within this culture, it has been proven time and time again that hard work and dedication simply don't matter when standing up against the administration's iron fist. The moment you step out of line, you're branded a traitor who can't and shouldn't be trusted. In the agency's eyes, you've committed the ultimate and unforgivable sin of telling the truth, *and thereby failed to put your administration, supervisor, and agency first.*

In the agency's eyes, the only acceptable position is that of blind allegiance and loyalty. If you dare to follow your own moral compass, your performance evaluations will reflect your treasonous ways. Your failure to accept any and all positions that your administration takes, regardless of the facts, regardless of what you've personally seen or heard, regardless of the truth, will result in you being blacklisted.

If you're not suspended or terminated, you'll feel the unspoken yet insidious retribution in numerous other ways. For no apparent reason, you'll be refused requests for lateral moves. When you apply for promotions, you'll be downgraded on your appraisal performances. Your various funding requests to help your families will start being denied without any reasonable or logical explanations, or you'll be demoted. And so it goes.

I worked a case involving a seven-year-old boy and his mother. His mother just couldn't get herself together and didn't work at her parenting and counseling programs. She lived by modest means and had nothing to her name. But God bless her, every single day she would get on her bicycle and travel many miles to see her son. Those two loved each other. When they were with one another, it was like they were in their own little world. It was very heartwarming.

The boy's foster parents wanted to adopt him. But he didn't want to be adopted. His mother was his mother and nobody else. I wanted to recommend legal guardianship, but my supervisor wouldn't let me. I was made to change my recommendation to adoption. The foster parents wanted a closed adoption, which meant they weren't going to let the child visit with his mother after the adoption became final. It wasn't the right decision.

I was called to testify by the attorney representing the mother. My supervisor told me I had to testify that adoption was the best permanent plan for this child. She stated it didn't matter what I felt; DCFS speaks with one voice. So I got up on the witness stand and testified that the child would be better off without his mother and that I felt he would be okay. Based on my testimony, the court ruled in the favor of DCFS and terminated the mother's parental rights.

I live with what I did every day of my life. I will never forgive myself. I wasn't courageous enough, and I sacrificed that little boy to save my own skin. I live with that every day. I did a terrible thing.

Now, you're not only living with a constant existential and moral crisis resulting from those times when you allowed your fear to silence you instead of speaking the truth and making the decision that you knew to be in the family's best interest. Unfortunately, you're now also living with a figurative gun pointed at you. Henceforth, you will remain in the crosshairs of an enraged administration. These realities that you now have to live with each and every day eat at you. You can almost feel the physical presence of this uninvited, unwelcomed intruder invading your spirit, tugging at your soul as you try to hold on just long enough to be free.

Far too many of us sit with our collective anger and self-loathing, asking God or some higher power to help us find a way out. We hope and pray for a way not to have to lie anymore, either by what we say or what we omit. Behind our silence lies our desperation:

I don't want to harm another family because of what I either say, don't say, or fail to do.

I can't stand to see another family harmed, abused by our agency. We're the good guys, right?

Please deliver me from this nightmare of conscience before I completely lose myself in the morass of moral indifference.

Can I forgive myself for going along, for standing by, because I needed to feed my family and because I was so very afraid? What must it be like to live and work without fear!

But now it's five, maybe ten years later, and I still sit in fearful silence. I'm trying to somehow mobilize enough courage to speak up. However, I remain silent, thinking to myself, trying over and over to convince myself, "Well, it's not me, I was simply representing the department."

"I'm not really responsible, I'm not to blame. I had no choice, right?"

Covert CSW Operatives

When it comes to court reports, many CSWs have developed tactical methods and coded language that help to covertly signal to the court that the truth behind the language and recommendations of a report is different—often far different—from what is written therein.

Hide and Seek

Say a mother tested positive in two random drug tests, one on April 3, 2010, and a second on September 9, 2011. The CSW has been told to include the following in the report:

> Mother has had a long and extensive history of substance abuse. She lost her children due to her chemical dependency issues. Mother's dirty tests illustrate that Mother continues to pose a risk to her children, and that she is not an appropriate caregiver at this time.

The CSW will often be told that he or she must include the following recommendations:

> DCFS recommends the following: Mother is ordered to continue with random drug testing. The children are to remain as placed in foster care. Mother's visits continue to be monitored.

In this all-too-typical example, the CSW is being told that he or she must emphasize negative statements and write the rest of the report in a way that ensures that the court comes away with the "obvious" conclusion that the mother is a hopeless "druggie" and should never get her kids back.

But the CSW also knows some other facts about this mother. This CSW has worked with this mother for more than eleven months and knows how much this mother loves her children, based on her consistent visits with her children and the CSWs observations during these visits. The CSW further knows that this mother has worked hard to comply with court orders and, for the most part, has been successful. This CSW additionally knows just how much the mother's daughter loves her, based on her daughter's behavior and statements during visits that the CSW or assigned staff observed.

The CSW also knows that the mother has been clean and sober for a verifiable period of eight months. Lastly, the CSW's experience, training, and time in the field tells her that relapse is a part of addiction recovery and must be viewed and assessed in context and not in a vacuum isolated from other relevant events.

Given these circumstances, the CSW, who is trying to stand up for the family without openly violating DCFS directives, often will find some place in the fifteen to twenty-plus pages of the report (not counting attachments) to sneak in additional factual statements that are also verifiably true about the mother. The CSW will try to do this in such a way that it will not be blatantly obvious, but at least allows the possibility of more truth reaching the court's attention.

So the CSW may include statements similar to the following:

> Mother also has had twenty-three consecutive clean tests after September 9, 2011. Mother has also maintained consistent visits with her child and was never observed to be under the influence during any visit. Mother has also worked very well with this CSW and continues to state and demonstrate that she is very committed to reunifying with her children. Mother additionally appears to love and be committed to her children's best interest. Mother and children have had and continue to have, based on all direct observations

and statements by children and mother, a strong bonded relationship.

The CSW also may add:

> The two dirty tests were missed tests, one because Mother admitted that she relapsed. Mother's father had died and she stated that she made a "terrible" mistake and used again. The second was due to a conflict with a court-ordered class, but this was worked out between the mother and CSW.

As true as these facts are, they run contrary to the department's position. However, if a CSW is able to carefully insert these positive and true aforementioned facts about the mother in the case, the family may have a fighting chance of being treated fairly if the court succeeds in reading between the lines. There is at least a possibility that because these particular facts seem so out of place and so contrary to the report's overall thrust and predominant recommendations, the court will notice the apparent inconsistency and ask questions that will reveal more of the truth in the case.

Typically the judges and referees will know that they are looking at a case in which another CSW covert operative is trying to reveal more of the truth about the mother. Hopefully, they will recognize that the CSW is almost certainly afraid but driven by principle to somehow get more of the truth to the courts. They will know that the CSW is compelled by conscience to attempt to ensure that the court can make the best possible, most informed decisions about the family in the case, so they might ask the CSW questions and look for body language or other cues. This has been a common and well-known practice among CSWs for years and years, and continues today in countless court reports.

If the CSWs buried truths are discovered before the report is submitted to the court, he or she may be directed to remove them by a supervisor, an ARA, or the RA, on orders from somewhere higher up (the RA is the highest level in this case). If the information the CSW had hoped to reveal in the report is removed by the decision of any one of these superiors, then the CSW will sometimes resort to Plan B.

Deep Throat

If CSWs can't discreetly write the truth into the report, they will sometimes make an anonymous call to an attorney opposing the department. CSWs may disguise their voices, go to an outside phone and call anonymously, or speak "off the record" if they trust the attorney. In this roundabout way, the attorney might alert the court to pivotal facts of the case that are missing or distorted in the report. Sometimes the attorney knows it's the CSW calling; sometimes he or she doesn't.

CSWs act covertly not to alter or embellish the truth, not to fabricate facts just because they feel sorry for their client, not because they aren't aware of how serious child abuse or neglect is, not because of inexperience, but simply because they are absolutely compelled to do so by their consciences. Their unimpeachable, principled convictions demand it. CSWs will sometimes find that they have no other alternative because they cannot and will not stand by and lie by omission when they feel that they must act on the family's behalf.

Cipher Method

Coded language is another very common method that CSWs use to write the truth into their reports. An example would be the following: First, the CSW will be told that he must write the following language and statements into his report, based on a typical hotline referral or, if involving an open case, statements made by some involved party that may or may not include family members:

> Father, according to his son and a neighbor witness, had repeatedly struck his son with a belt and yelled profanities

at him. His son, according to the same neighbor, was afraid and ran to his home for shelter and refused to return home. The neighbor then called in a Child Abuse Hotline referral.

The CSW also knows, after doing some fact-finding and further investigation, that the reason that father spanked his son with a belt was because he had been shooting a BB gun at his little sister, whom he occasionally used as target practice. This CSW also knows that this same boy often runs to his neighbor's home, trying to avoid taking responsibility for his transgressions and failing to abide by his father's rules.

But if the department's position, which may be taken by a supervisor or the ARA, is to ensure that an allegation of physical abuse is sustained by the court, the CSW will be told to edit the report to only include the statements that will help guarantee the conclusion that a young boy was terrorized by an out-of-control father, and the boy must be removed from his father's custody.

The following cipher may be attempted by the CSW to try and include a contextually, factually accurate account of what took place. This CSW may write the following:

> Father, according to his son and neighbor witness, had repeatedly spanked his son with a belt for shooting a BB gun at his little sister, and had raised his voice in an angry fashion, yelling disapproval and some profanities at his son. According to the same neighbor who voiced concerns about the son and father, the son appeared afraid and subsequently ran into the neighbor's home, which he apparently had done before to avoid punishment, and stated that he didn't want to go home and was afraid to face his father.

The CSW hopes that this version, as opposed to the first version, will be allowed to remain in the court report and that the court will decipher the coded language and glean the additional facts necessary to form a contextual, factually based understanding of what took place, so the court can make an informed and just ruling.

CSWs live under the ubiquitous threat of punishment for not following the department line at all costs. So, they will use this and other methods to try and report more facts and, ultimately, the truth.

Hot Seat

This fourth technique is by far the most distressing, frightening, and traumatizing for a CSW. This is when a CSW is subpoenaed to testify in a case. The CSW's supervisor or somebody higher up has told the CSW that he or she represents the department and so must say x, y, and z. They tell the CSW that he or she is relieved of any personal responsibility because, after all, the CSW represents the department and "the department speaks with one voice."

The CSW had already tried Hide and Seek, but someone directly above or somewhere up the chain of command found it and had it removed. The CSW didn't have the time or chance to safely use Deep Throat, and the Cipher Method almost worked, but at the last second a superior told the CSW to "clean up some language" because of an "apparent inconsistency in tone" and said that the report had "too many unnecessary facts, which makes the department look inconsistent." So the CSW, having exhausted all previous methods, feels like he or she failed the family and violated his or her moral code to tell the truth, thus sacrificing integrity.

The court day arrives. Secretly, the CSW hopes and prays that the case is continued, postponed, or somehow dismissed. Or, best of all that the court will tell the CSW that he or she is no longer needed and excused from appearing. With no such luck, the CSW sits in court and is called to the stand. But first comes the oath "to tell the truth, the whole truth, and nothing but the truth so help me God." And the CSW thinks, *You must be kidding. If I did that, I'd be history. I'd be fired so fast, I wouldn't have time to collect my personal pictures in my cubicle.*

But the CSW is compelled to do something. The CSW initially responds to questions in accordance with the department's position, but before he or she can utter the required incomplete or misleading "facts," the court interrupts and asks to know the CSW's personal, professional observations and assessments, i.e., the truth. Then the CSW dares to tell the truth.

The CSW looks over to the county's counsel, who is glaring at the CSW in such a way that if looks could kill, the CSW would have been killed, buried, and exhumed only to be killed and buried again. The CSW starts worrying. As the CSW experiences mounting distress and terror, trying not to show it outwardly, he or she wonders, *what happens now?*

The CSW knows that even the truth doesn't provide any guarantee that the court will rule in any certain direction. The court will make what it believes to be the lawful and just decision on all matters that come before it. But the CSW knows, with absolute certainty, that the chances of the court making decisions and rulings that are accurate, just, reasonable, and fair are almost nil if the court is denied the truth, the whole truth, and nothing but the truth.

Later, the CSW can tell his or her superiors "I was so ordered" to speak the truth in court, but he or she will still face repercussions. In order of likelihood, the CSW's punishment will be: ostracized by management, harassment, intense and unrelenting scrutiny, threatened with insubordination, not getting a promotion, denied lateral transfer requests, suspended, or worse terminated. In rare circumstances, he or she will experience no repercussions.

And so the CSW did his or her best, took chances, and took on personal risk to do the right thing. The CSW can only hope that it was worth it.

The Consequences of Refusing to Go Along

You're called into that dreaded administrator's office and the fear starts to take hold. This is not the kind of fear that comes from making a serious legitimate mistake; that type of fear makes sense and you can deal with it. No, this fear is borne out of something much more insidious, mind-twisting, and tormenting. This is the fear that you've been caught red-handed violating the one inexcusable, unwritten, and unforgivable law: telling the truth. But you hope against hope, as you slow your gait and get closer to that office, that maybe this time they'll see the reality, the truth, and it'll be okay. Maybe . . .

But as you get closer to that office, you find yourself starting to silently scream inside, *Please don't tell me that I can't tell the truth! Not this time, I can't, not again! Please don't tell me that I have to slam these parents when I know they didn't do anything wrong! Please don't! I can't! I just can't lie! I won't! I won't!*

You hold back the tears but your eyes redden nonetheless and now look bloodshot. Your palms start to sweat, but you quickly rub them against your clothes.

You walk in.

Your nightmare is confirmed. Once again, you're told that you saw it wrong, that you didn't hear what you thought you heard, that you're just not seeing it right, that the department's position is this and that you need to remember that you represent the department. Therefore, you need to write this.

"But that's not the truth." Your response is barely discernible. You muster the courage and utter, "I'm not going to write that. It's not the truth. I won't. I won't hang these parents out to dry."

Then you hear those penetrating, cutting, and frightening words: "You're going to be insubordinate." Suddenly your world seems surreal, yet all too real and familiar. You've been through this before, and déjà vu is uncomfortable.

You try not to let your quickly mounting fear show. You somehow know instinctively that if they see you afraid, if they see you sweat, the threats and attacks for insisting on telling the truth will only get worse.

Then the almost suffocating scrutiny comes. You half expected it, but you're still caught off guard. Your supervisor is great. But his boss (ARA) and her boss (RA) keep the pressure on, and it's relentless. You know why they're doing it, but that brings little to no relief. The fear and pressure mount. You've always been a great employee, but now your evaluations are marked down. Why? Just because you told the truth, because you wouldn't write what you knew wasn't true. Everything you do, everything you write, and every decision you make are now constantly second-guessed.

You begin to question yourself under the intense, unrelenting, and all-consuming pressure, the constant innuendos and indirect and blatant statements that you're not a good social worker and that you don't know what you're doing. The suffocating scrutiny over everything you touch starts to take its toll. *Didn't I do the right thing? Wasn't I supposed to tell the truth? They were telling me to lie. I can't, I just can't. I won't.*

Now the self-doubt starts to creep in. It's slow at first but steadily grows. It takes hold. Now it haunts you. You start to feel different. You feel different about everything.

You're becoming more irritable at work and at home. You're not sleeping. *Didn't I do the right thing? Was I wrong? Did I miss something? Why are they so angry? Why are they so adamant to the point of threatening me and tormenting me with this suffocating scrutiny? Why are they doing this to me? I'm a good worker, I am, I am. God, I wish it would stop. Got to hang on. I won't sell my soul.*

The next morning, you think, *I hate coming here, I hate it.* You never used to feel that way. And yet the incessant internal chatter continues unabated and loudly: *How I dread and hate coming here. Got to make this stop. I'm a good worker, I know what I'm doing, don't I?*

You start taking anti-anxiety pills. You come to work and wear your unhappiness like a set of prison garb that you can't take off or exchange. Your leadership has told you repeatedly that you're not seeing and hearing reality right. It's becoming impossible to distinguish what is real and what isn't. The damage is done. You're breaking down physically, emotionally. Your spirit is tired, so tired, and weakening.

Must hang on. Got to hang on. I have to feed my children, I need my job. My family depends on me. I am a good worker, but why don't I feel that way anymore? I used to, but that once unflappable feeling and belief that I was a damn good worker who cares deeply for my families and works tirelessly for them is fading now.

Each day that you come in, the little evidence that you were ever good at what you did and what you cared about disappears further. Your inner voice, once your staunchest and most dependable advocate, is now an unexpected accomplice in your growing self-doubt and barrages you constantly with undermining queries: *Do I know really know my job? I thought I did, didn't I? I was good at what I did, wasn't I? Did I miss something?*

One day, you come to work not remembering how good you once felt about yourself as a social worker. There's no evidence around you. It's all been stripped away. All that remains are statements and innuendos from the very leaders you look to for recognition. No positive feedback is forthcoming. You're blacklisted, on the outside, exiled from anything acceptable and trustworthy.

You hear your inner voice: *I'm a bad worker, the one who doesn't listen and do as told.*

Then, somewhere deep in the recesses of your very being, you hear something that sounds strangely familiar, although you can't remember from when:

It wasn't the truth, dammit. It wasn't. I won't.

The New Normal

I'm reminded of when I worked as a therapist at a federal prison during my graduate school program. I was luckier than most because this internship paid surprisingly well (many of them did not) and provided me with a great opportunity to experience and work with a myriad of moderate-to-serious clinical issues.

I further honed my skills by providing group and individual therapy, which gave me an opportunity to have experiences with a very unique and special population, our locked-away population. I learned a great deal from these men. I never could have received these moments from any textbook or theorist. Our clients provided some of the most important keys that helped deepen our understanding and empathy and afforded us tremendous insight into human behavior and the human condition.

The reason I'm reminded of this job is because, among the many clinical experiences I've had and cherish, two in particular stand out and illustrate this chapter's main focus. I call these two experiences "Alpha-Omega" and "Solitary."

Alpha-Omega

My immediate supervisor at the prison was an African-American woman who was the prison's licensed psychologist. Her name, no kidding, was Dr. Alpha-Omega. The prison had a population of about four to five hundred men. Dr. Alpha-Omega and I were the only therapists who provided direct psycho-therapeutic services to the prison population. The good doctor was usually very busy with many other administrative matters, and that left me to handle most of the actual therapy and the direct services. That didn't bother me a bit, as I was very grateful for the learning opportunity and ended up loving every minute of it. I gained a wealth of knowledge and grew tremendously as a clinician.

Only weeks into my new position was I asked to attend a board meeting. About twenty minutes into it, Dr. Alpha-Omega suddenly let out the loudest, most thunderous, most blood-curdling scream that I had ever personally witnessed or seen on any TV or movie screen. I immediately went into duck-and-cover mode, almost certain that mayhem was about to ensue.

As I looked around, I was amazed to see that not a soul had moved, not even an inch. No one even blinked an eye. There wasn't even the slightest outward recognition of something that almost caused me to jump out of my skin and into cardiac arrest. They just kept talking and continued with the meeting.

At some point, I caught the good doctor's gaze. She gave me a reassuring smile and very discreetly nodded her head as if to say, "I'm okay and sorry for startling you."

Whenever she felt stress, Dr. Alpha-Omega would, without any warning or apparent provocation, release a primal, earth-shaking scream that I thought would awaken the dead.

The warden, the department heads, and the entire prison population simply got used to it. It became a normal part of their shared environmental landscape, as common as the sun rising and setting. It became part of their "new normal."

We humans have an incredible capacity to get used to stuff, even when the stuff isn't necessarily wanted, healthy, or positive, and even when we dread it, fear it, resent it, and wish it wasn't present in our lives.

Too many CSWs, past, present, and most likely future, experience primal-scream moments in their DCFS worlds. But they don't have the luxury of a Dr. Alpha-Omega to help make concrete sense of it, and their primal-scream experiences are not as innocuous. No, our primal-scream moments are silent yet equally deafening and result in varying degrees of trauma and harm. They're just as unsettling and frightening, but build at a much slower pace. They're just as impactful, but their delivery is seldom expressed as publicly and dramatically as the good doctor's. They're insidious, stealthy, and very carefully dispensed.

I sat with one CSW who, after reading "A Confession," started to tear up, her eyes becoming so red it was now hard to see their natural color. Then she shared her story.

She had worked with a family that had one daughter who lived at home and one older teenage boy who had been placed out of the home. This CSW had worked extensively with this family and concluded that the teenage boy was simply "working the system." He didn't have any legitimate or verifiable "at-risk" reasons for not being home. He simply didn't want to deal with the family's rules about curfew, normal parental expectations, and appropriate consequences for misbehaving. This kid wanted the freedom and all the privileges of an adult without the responsibilities or consequences.

Several other CSWs saw the same thing. But the RA told the CSW that she had no choice but to nail the parents in her report. She tried over and over to tell him that the parents didn't do anything wrong. They were simply trying to be good parents and were very confused and frustrated that the department seemed to be emboldening their son to behave incorrigibly and immaturely, seemingly conspiring to allow their son to get his way.

This RA kept telling this CSW that the department had already taken a position and that she must conform to it and make the parents look bad. The CSW held her own and said with fear and much anxiety, "No, I won't, I can't do it. It's not true. These parents didn't do anything wrong."

The CSW, in a resolute and defiant voice, with tears in her eyes, told me that she didn't write what she was told to write. She said that she would never sell her soul and sell out. No job, title, or money would be worth that for her.

When the CSW shared her story with her close colleagues, friends at work, and supervisor, she had her Dr. Alpha-Omega primal-scream moment. No one was surprised or shocked. No one even flinched; no one needed to duck and cover. Her cohorts simply shared that they too had experienced similar issues or knew of people who had endured the same treatment, all because they were requested to set aside their integrity or something similar.

Many months later, I saw how the CSW was clearly still shaken by what had happened. She was still paying the price because her RA threatened her by saying, "If you don't, you're going to be insubordinate." After that, every move she made and every word she wrote on every case she touched was closely scrutinized, reviewed, challenged, and even censored or altered. Her supervisor was very sympathetic but essentially powerless to stop or filter out much of what she was going through. He knew that he could just as easily also be accused of being insubordinate if he didn't obey his supervising administrators. This wasn't the first time he found himself in this moral bind or the first time he had to watch a CSW or another supervisor endure it.

This CSW went on to say that after weeks of working under the microscope, she knew that if she did anything that wasn't absolutely perfect, she would be giving them an opening for immediate exploitation and worse.

Then, as if things weren't already almost emotionally intolerable for her, her RA called her into his office one morning and told her that she was now under investigation by Internal Affairs (IA), affectionately known in our DCFS culture as the "goon squad." He told her that it was regarding a child death that occurred two years ago, and that she had been one of the last CSWs to "touch the case."

When a child's death occurs in a CSW's caseload, certain things happen almost immediately. The CSW starts to feel the panic and fear. *Oh my God. Did I do everything I should have? Did I cross every T and dot every I? Did I miss anything? Could I have somehow prevented it or helped to prevent it?* The CSW also know that he or she will come under intense, indifferent, relentless, and punishing scrutiny.

CSWs also know that they'll get a call from IA. When they do, it's absolutely frightening and instantly shatters what little feeling of safety exists in our culture of fear. It's like you're suddenly thrust into a dark tunnel filled with the most frightening sounds imaginable, but it's dark and you can't quite make out what exactly the sounds are or where they're coming from.

Then what she shared next was my Dr. Alpha-Omega moment with her. She said that she just couldn't stop worrying about what was happening with IA, that it was emotionally crushing her. This, combined with the scrutiny that she was already under, was reaching a breaking point. She knew, as we all do, that many CSWs and some supervisors, but never RAs or ARAs or other managers, have been fired and seriously disciplined after an IA investigation.

She said she kept asking her RA about what was going on with her IA investigation but got nowhere. Then she tried asking her ARA what was going on. To her surprise, her ARA said that she wasn't aware of an IA investigation but that they were probably just very busy and hadn't yet contacted her.

The CSW said she went back to waiting, but after a few more weeks she just couldn't stand it anymore. She called Internal Affairs herself and asked what the status was on her investigation.

Then came the reply: "What investigation?"

Her RA had made it up. As she told me this, we both shed some tears, which we followed with silence. Her story didn't shock me or surprise me. I didn't even move an inch. It had long since become our "new normal."

I'm not sure how or when it happened, but at some point, we needed to add "PR agent" to our duty list and make time to craft clever yet hollow talking points for the media. Looking deeply into familial issues and finding a solution is far too complicated to be turned into an impersonal, cold, cost-benefit business decision. When did it start becoming a crime to speak up and disagree with our leadership? When did it become a crime for the leadership to admit to making mistakes and fix them to really help our case families? The family dynamic is just that: dynamic and fluid. Vital, large, and complicated, each family unit has its own science, language, culture, and context. To demand perfect, scripted outcomes by playing fast and loose with the truth is at best impossible and at worst a great, damning disservice to the families that we supposedly help.

Doing the right thing is always hard. Let us not make it impossible.

The prevailing and overriding belief is: *I'm an RA, you're a CSW, our department has taken a position, and you must support it and conform.* Much of our DCFS culture has done this for so long and so often without any effective checks and balances or accountability that it has become a very normal, commonplace practice, one of our many primal-scream moments. It's just another part of our "new normal."

But at what cost?

Solitary

Three months into my time working at the prison, I was asked to perform strip searches and cavity checks. That was the last thing I'd ever expected to be doing, and I was seriously not prepared for it. Apart from what I'd seen in a few comedies over the years—and even then the situation was only implied—I had no idea what to do or expect.

There were ten inmates. Thankfully, they all knew the drill and had no issues with it. I walked into the designated men's restroom and one by one they came in, dropped the pants, bent over, and coughed, showing me all their body cavities. No undergraduate or graduate class had prepared me for this. I learned quickly that when you work at a prison, it's standard procedure for all to be cross-trained to handle most if not all responsibilities and duties in case a riot breaks out or some kind of emergency occurs.

One in particular, who I'll call James, was about six foot two and looked like he had been a bodybuilder for several years. He didn't have the hard edge, though, that many of the inmates to whom I had met and provided therapeutic services did. James was also articulate.

Thankfully, the visuals went by quickly. A few days later, I was surprised to learn that James had been placed into solitary confinement. James seemed even-tempered and had said that he just wanted to do his time and avoid any trouble. I asked what had happened and what he had done, and the watch captain told me that James hadn't done anything wrong. So, I asked, why then was he in solitary confinement? The watch captain said that he had gotten word that a close relative had died, and it was standard practice that whenever an inmate experienced a major loss, they're automatically and quickly put into solitary confinement "for their own good."

I was pissed. This went against common sense and everything I had learned in my training and education as a clinician. To isolate a person at such a critical juncture was absolutely cruel, inhumane, and unacceptable. I immediately went to where James was confined and spent the better part of a couple hours there, just listening to him. When someone has experienced the loss of a loved one, you don't need to know what to say; listening and caring will do. The next day, I spoke to Dr. Alpha-Omega, and then had a long chat with the warden. I requested that I or some other supportive, appropriate, and compassionate staff member be called to support all future inmates when they experienced a major loss, and that no inmate going forward should ever be isolated at a time when he needs someone's support.

DCFS has a form of solitary confinement with its CSWs and sometimes their supervisors. The most profound, disturbing, and sometimes permanently life-altering experience that a CSW can have is when a child on his or her caseload dies or when a CSW has been involved for some time in a long-term case in which a child attempts or commits suicide. Anyone who does this work long enough will go through or know of someone who will go through this terrifying nightmare.

There are two salient reasons why our version of solitary is so devastating for our CSWs and supervisors. First, we CSWs have our own vicarious traumatization (VT) to deal with. Our VT (as I explain in great detail in the chapter on vicarious traumatization) predisposes CSWs to have a tremendously heightened sense of guilt when tragic things happen to their case families, even if the tragedy is self-imposed, as in the case of suicide. CSWs that haven't had the time or agency support—and most haven't—are at risk for tremendous yet unjustified self-blame. This self-blame, if left unaddressed, as is usually the case, can and often does lead to self-loathing. This is especially damaging because of how our agency traditionally responds to child deaths.

I wish I could say that it was hard to find an example of how our agency responds, but it isn't. A supervisor, who I'll call Sam, shared her story with me. She had been a supervisor for several years and was well respected for her social work and supervisory skills and her unquestionable commitment to the welfare of her case families and the CSWs under her control.

Sam had just received a prestigious community award for her work with DCFS. She was very proud and grateful for the recognition, as it was a complete surprise to her. In our DCFS culture, internal or external recognition is very rare.

At this time, Sam was juggling two units based out of two different offices. She had some Spanish-speaking workers, although she didn't speak Spanish. But she had some CSWs who were fluent in Spanish. I'll call one of them Jorge.

Jorge investigated one particular referral alleging abuse of two kids, a five-year-old girl and her seven-year-old brother. They were living with their paternal grandmother, who spoke only Spanish. Their mother had been released from jail after a recent incarceration that had nothing to do with child abuse or neglect. The father's whereabouts were unknown. The mother could speak English and Spanish.

Jorge's investigation included speaking with the children, their paternal grandmother, and the mother. He also talked with all available collateral contacts. In the end, Jorge couldn't find any facts or evidence that supported the allegations of abuse and neglect and recommended closing the referral as "unsubstantiated." Sam also reviewed the case and came to the same conclusion as Jorge. She closed the referral.

Sam felt strongly that because of past referrals and the family's meager economic means, it was important to make some kind of referral so that the mother would receive free family counseling services to help her when she became stressed. The mother had stated on the referral that she appreciated these counseling services, which were part of a program that at the time was called Alternative Response. Alternative Response was used with some closed referrals in which concerns remained but there wasn't enough evidence to open a case and file a petition for child abuse and neglect with the court.

Sam notified her ARA about her decision to close this referral with Alternative Response in place. Sam was also told that the family would be immediately contacted and the family counseling services would start quickly.

About two weeks later, Sam learned from a chance encounter with the contact person for the requested services that the family hadn't been receiving services. This upset Sam, and she quickly tried calling the mother. A man answered, apparently a boyfriend. Sam was unaware that the mother had a boyfriend, as she had recently been released from jail and hadn't mentioned that she had a boyfriend or serious relationship.

The mother's boyfriend said that she would be back later. Sam called several more times that night with no luck.

The next day, Sam came into the office, saw a picture of the five-year-old in the newspaper, and almost passed out. The girl had apparently been brutally beaten and molested. In the article, a county supervisor said that it was one of the worst cases of child abuse he had ever heard of and that the CSW and the supervisor may face criminal charges. The mother's boyfriend allegedly had done this.

Within twenty-four hours, Sam was called into one of her ARA's offices. This ARA wasn't her direct boss but had been told that he needed to quickly speak with her. This ARA and Sam had a good working relationship.

This ARA told Sam, "I'm putting you on desk duty." Sam didn't understand, so she asked what it meant, and for how long and why. The ARA, appearing very uncomfortable, answered, "I don't know," to all of Sam's anxious queries. "I don't have any more information."

The ARA told Sam that she could no longer have contact with any children and couldn't have any cases involving children. Sam asked, "What am I supposed to do?"

Sam found herself on desk duty for eight agonizing and psychologically punishing months. Not only that, but her desk was the most visible in the entire office. Because she was kept in the dark about why she had been placed on desk duty and was just told that the matter was under investigation, the fear of what may or may not happen to her job took its toll.

Sam said that she kept herself together when she was in the office, but when she went out to her car for breaks or lunch, she would cry in pain, relentless embarrassment, and humiliation at what her work life had become. The fear of not knowing what was going to happen felt unbearable. She took to impulse-feeding just to survive emotionally and psychologically. She felt so hopeless that on more than one occasion she contemplated homicide and suicide, which scared her.

Sam said that many caring CSWs shared their sympathies with her. Some expressed anger at what the administration was doing to her. But many other CSWs and supervisors would walk by and be careful not to make eye contact or speak with her. Sam said that she felt like she had become a leper, like she had contracted some contagion and, for some unknown and unjustified reason, had been quarantined. She had become a pariah. Sam found herself in the DCFS version of solitary confinement.

Sam said that some CSWs would tell her, "You're going to kill yourself to stay here," to which she would reply, "I won't give them the satisfaction."

One day while in her wall-free dungeon, she thought about what she still could do to help her case families and her fellow CSWs. A light came on. She decided to update all the office resources that CSWs access and make available to their families. She knew, as we all do, that our resource lists are real hit-and-miss affairs. No one really has the time to keep them current or even eliminate providers who aren't still in business.

Sam had found a way to still help our case families and be productive, something that she desperately needed.

One day while Sam was well into her new project, her ARA—who still hadn't offered or shared even one single word of sympathy or support—found out that she had gone to help a grateful CSW detain three children. Sam had been very careful not to say anything during the detainment, and had only acted as another pair of hands.

Her boss called her into her office and immediately began to drill her. "What are you doing?" she demanded. Sam shared details about her resource project and all the progress she was making.

With an indignant and irritated voice, Sam's boss simply dismissed her resource project and confronted her about helping the CSW with detaining the three kids: "You're not supposed to have any contact with kids. You're not supposed to have any interaction with families. You are not to have any phone contact."

Sam, now feeling more indignation and humiliation than fear, repeated a question she had asked months before: "What am I supposed to do, then?" Her boss replied, "I don't have anything for you at this time, but I'll let you know when I have something that you can do."

At this point, Sam still knew nothing about the status of her investigation. She had endured months with absolutely no feedback. When Sam and Jorge finally had their formal investigative review meeting with several ARAs and other DCFS officials, they learned nothing. One agency official asked her if she wanted any support, which she found self-serving and offered only for the agency's own CYA ("Cover Your Ass") purposes; this official had never before asked her how she was doing and did not offer any follow-up during or after the meeting.

One thing was clear though, and it's something that all CSWs, and often their supervisors, figure out really fast: when a problem arises, you're alone and dangling in the wind.

At one point, Sam's ARA handed her a list of assignments. They were menial tasks that some of the other supervisors said that Sam could do. Some of Sam's supervisors were upset that they had gotten stuck with Sam's workload and sought some thinly veiled payback.

One item stood out like a sore thumb. It read, "Organize

children's room." It translated as, "Go clean the kids' waiting room." Feeling even more humiliated but becoming righteously angry, she challenged her boss about this assignment. Her boss quickly asked Sam if she thought it was "demeaning."

Sam just stopped and paused. Then she looked up and said, "No, I don't *think* it's demeaning, I *know* it's demeaning, and I won't tolerate it!"

After eight months, she finally received another formal assignment.

Sam's story has been playing out for years and continues to be part of our culture's status quo of profound and unconscionable indifference. It's one of the ways in which we treat and mistreat each other.

To suddenly be told to stop doing your job with very little or no explanation, and then be told you have to just sit is the way DCFS responds to a child's death. To not be offered any formal or informal words of consolation, concern, or support from your administration or your bosses is what CSWs and many supervisors have lived with and continue to endure.

How an agency so full of individuals who possess advanced degrees in human behavior and psychology, who have spent years working with people in pain and fear with complex life circumstances, could fail to understand their inherent and ethical responsibility to provide immediate and ongoing support for their own is beyond words. How we can choose to abandon and neglect our own at a time when they're facing such tremendous fear, uncertainty, humiliation, and inner turmoil orchestrated by our own bureaucratic hands is unthinkable. The "new normal" is where the grass stops being green and trees no longer grow vertically.

At what cost?

A Time We Got It Right

I was about to give up hope of doing real social work. The frustration of trying to do so over and over only to end up running into seemingly endless roadblocks left me feeling a growing sense of hopelessness. I wanted to quit so many times. I felt so much despair over being unable to really help families, make a difference in their lives, and do what I thought I was going to spend a career doing. I wanted to work for the kind of employer that valued and prioritized respect and genuine support of case families and clients, that truly believed in the *actual* "best interest of our families" and did not just use the phrase "the best interest" as a platitude or some sort of politically correct company line.

Fortunately, throughout my long career I have enjoyed what I call "social work moments" (SWM). These were the moments when I could really help clients. They were very rare and far too infrequent. But they helped sustain me and keep me going, helping me believe that maybe things would improve. That maybe when we got new supervisors, managers, and directors, we would finally usher in the change we desperately wanted.

I developed solid working relationships with my families based on mutual respect and dignity, genuine interest in their welfare, a clear understanding of their issues, and real empathy for their well-being. These SWMs allowed me to take a symbolic deep breath of oxygen, which I knew I needed to hold on to for as long as possible because I knew it would be a long time before I could take another breath.

One day, when I felt like I was losing that oxygen, a colleague told me about a new program called Family Group Decision

Making (FGDM). The colleague told me some unbelievable things about this program. Families were able to develop their own case plans during genuinely family centered conferences, so that they could take the lead in addressing the issues raised by DCFS. Those conferences were coordinated for families around their schedules at times, days and venues that were comfortable and felt safe for them. And because these conferences ran about four hours, we even provided a meal. Incredible!

I couldn't believe what I was hearing. Could a program like this really exist in the DCFS culture? A culture, like so many bureaucracies, that isn't known for willingly giving up its power or control over the families that come through the system?

I was absolutely intrigued and cautiously hopeful for the first time in a very long time. Maybe, just maybe, this program was real and not just political window dressing, as so many other programs were. Maybe I was going to be able to do real social work. Maybe I could have the career I had always envisioned. I started frantically calling anyone and everyone, trying to find out as much as I could about FGDM.

I learned that FGDM was in its last trial phase. I later discovered that our then powers to be which were our then-director, our then dependency court, multiple managers, deputy directors and other bigwig community partners and stakeholders were all pushing for FDGM. What was most incredible and improbable to me was that it was our then supervising dependency court judge, Terry Freedman, who was the biggest lobbyist and advocate for FGDM. You see our dependency court was and is the very symbol and pinnacle of power and control for us social workers.

Our dependency court system, like any other court system, has an inherent adversarial design pitting one attorney against another, with a win at all costs built in prime directive. So to hear that it's then leader, top dog who holds (and is) the most powerful position in our DCFS child welfare world, Judge Freedman was the champion of advocating to implement FDGM, a program who's main focus and purpose was to give up power and control to the family, well it was unbelievable.

The FGDM model was ingenious in its simplicity, and was potentially life-altering and transformational in its design. Its design endorsed every value and principle that I had idealistically hoped to find in a place where I was seeking to help people. A very important ingredient in the foundation for this model was based on a construct called "Strength Based."

For as long as most of my seasoned colleagues can remember, we social workers and many other helping professions have always had a deficit mind-set when it comes to our case families. This means that we have been trained and indoctrinated for decades to see and relate to our families through their deficits, i.e., their mistakes, misjudgments, and wrong choices. So when we try and talk with our families, we social workers will say things such as, "Well, you know what you did," or "Based on the choice you made," or "So, what do you think about what you did?" or "Why did you chose that?" or "You have to do this to make up for that . . ."

We relate to our case families in this way even when we draft case plans for them. We essentially create what amounts to a to-do list, which they must follow—or else. We quite literally have told and most of the time continue to tell families, "If you don't finish your to-do list, you'll never get your kids back," essentially falling into the trap of seeing only the deficits in our families. This also is often referred to as the "medical model," which says that *I, your social worker, know what's wrong with you, and I know what exactly what you need to do, or else.*

A strength-based framework is the complete antitheses of this antiquated, profoundly disrespectful, and arrogant deficit-minded approach. It emphasizes the importance of and need to first notice, listen to, and acknowledge the strength of the person or family with whom you're working. Not just to establish rapport and some bridge for communication (although it certainly will do those things), but most importantly because this approach believes that resolutions are based on strengths. The vast majority of people reach for their strengths to address and overcome their life challenges, concerns, and obstacles. So, applying this principle through a strength-based practice is simply Human Beings 101.

While the term "strength-based" at the time was new to me, the underlying principles were not. They were very much akin to who I was, and hoped to remain, as a professional and a person.

These were the FGDM principles:

I.   **Families as experts** (about themselves).

II. **Your own family as your best guide** (with "family" defined as anyone and everyone, blood-linked or not, who knows and loves the children and supports them and the family's welfare).

III. **Respect for families** (the ability to see a family and appreciate its position and culture to develop and maintain respect).

IV. **Families as primary decision makers** (to allow them to empower themselves—if anyone outside the family makes a decision for them, it might not be followed).

V.   **Mistakes as opportunities for growth and development** (to identify and understand behaviors as expressions of unmet needs).

VI. **Resolutions are based on strengths** (such as talents, gifts, and areas of our lives we can fall back on).

VII. **Celebration of differences** (understanding where the family comes from, why it thinks the way it does, and its common experiences, with the purpose of understanding them and not assuming we know them just by their external characteristics).

The more I learned, the more I grew excited. I couldn't believe that maybe I had found my social work niche. To work with people with genuine respect, not judgment; with dignity, not condescension; and in our words, tones, and hearts.

FGDMs were basically family conferences where the family members ("family" as defined in FGDM Principle II) gathered. All the participants were mobilized around a very specific, succinct, and predetermined purpose statement.

Key family members crafted this statement as the family conference was being coordinated. All participants knew about the purpose statement and agreed to it before coming to the conference. This was a critical part of the FGDM coordination process, and provided all participants with a clear and singular focus.

One of the amazing aspects of an FGDM family conference, the thing that set it apart from all other conference models currently in use in our vast child and family welfare industry, was that it was a family meeting that agency representatives attended, *not* an agency meeting that some family members attended. This nuanced yet beautifully simple distinction is massively important when you're working with families in the system. This is the foundation of the FGDM's design, principles, and values, which is critical to its success with our case families.

When one attends an FGDM, he or she is basically being *invited* into the family's living room and, by extension, into their intimate and private world. In this philosophy, it is an honor and privilege to be granted such permission and access, and I was fortunate enough—and remain so very grateful to this day—to receive hundreds and hundreds of invitations.

The FGDM conference model was based on the following family-focused, strength-based, structured agenda:

Welcome and family's special traditional opening, if family has one

Many families start with a prayer, poem, song, or some words from an elder or community leader.

Self-introduction

One by one, the participants introduce themselves and explain their relation to the family and why they're there. This decreases anxiety.

Explanation of the suggested family conference guidelines

The focus should be on the agreed-to purpose statement. There is no shaming or blaming; everyone has a right to be respected, everyone is important, and everyone will get a turn to speak, with the understanding that everything shared will remain private. The CSW will ask the family if it has any other suggested rules before asking, "May I have your permission to enforce these guidelines?"

It's okay to respectively disagree

The CSW clarifies that it is okay to voice opinions, but without attacking or defending.

Clarification of the family's purpose

The conference's purpose statement should be short and clear. In many cases, the family conference's purpose is to decide where and with whom the children are going to live, as well as a back-up plan.

Explanation and execution of three phases:

1) *Sharing strengths and concerns.* In that order, everyone specifically addresses and focuses on the agreed-to conference purpose.

2) *Family alone time.* All non-family participants must leave the room to allow family members to discuss the shared concerns of all participants, including the DCFS representative. Then the family creates a plan that specifically addresses all child-welfare concerns that appear in the family-crafted purpose statement.

3) *Presentation of family plan.* Everyone returns to the conference room, at which time the DCFS representative is presented with the family plan, and the agent must agree to and approve the plan (which often comes after some discussion and negotiation).

Thanks to all participants, closing of family conference

The foundational values of FDGM were another important ingredient that I continue to practice to this day in all my professional work with my case families and clients:

I.   Families have strengths and can change.

II. Strengths are what ultimately resolve concerns.

III. Strengths are discovered through listening, noticing, and paying attention to people.

IV. Strengths are enhanced when they are acknowledged and encouraged.

V.   People gain a sense of hope when they are heard.

VI. Options are preferable to advice. Advice is basically disrespectful.

VII. Empowering people is preferable to controlling them.

VIII. A consultant is more helpful to people then a boss.

It continues to puzzle and sadden me and many of my colleagues that these still aren't the values that drive the decisions of DCFS and its interactions with families.

A consortium of DCFS, court, and community leaders picked from an SPA (service providing area) in Los Angeles County participated in the program's trial run.

This was when I got my first live glimpse of FGDM in action, and I couldn't believe what I was seeing and experiencing. It was magical and transformational. It was like I had stepped into a different agency, one that talked to families in a completely different way.

I attended my first FGDM family conference in 2001 and remember it like it was yesterday. The first thing that struck me was that it was at night, which was when the entire family could come. The second thing was that we provided food. Oh my God! We were actually breaking bread with the family. Wow! For DCFS to show that level of consideration and thoughtfulness made me wonder, *Is this really DCFS? Where am I? Is this some sort of outside group that we hired to coordinate and facilitate this? This can't be us.* For DCFS to understand and incorporate this simple yet rich and powerful tradition was incredible to witness. The universal role that breaking bread played and continues to play in all our cultures is so huge. And FGDM got it!

The next thing that impressed me was the location: a public library conference room. For the family, this was a friendly and familiar venue. This site selection completely changed the conference's feeling and atmosphere from the usual "under the microscope/interrogation" feeling and an "anything you say can and will be used against you" atmosphere to "it's okay and it's safe—we're in our community."

I watched the conference, riveted. There was a conference facilitator and co-facilitator. The facilitator was from DCFS but was completely impartial and did not represent the agency; a separate social worker did that. The facilitator's role was to enforce the guidelines, ensure that the agenda was followed, and keep the focus on the family-crafted purpose statement. It respectfully kept everyone focused and on track. The co-facilitator took notes on a large easel everyone could see, thus serving as the "family historian."

What happened at the start of the family conference was something that I had never witnessed before in all my years with DCFS, which at that time was six years. The facilitator very respectfully asked the family if it would like to start its family conference with a traditional opening. This particular family chose to say a prayer out loud. This set the tone for the entire meeting.

As the facilitator started with the first phase, the sharing of strengths and concerns, I was fascinated by the power and necessity of taking the time to have all participants notice and acknowledge their strengths to one another. I remembered Operational Principle VI: *Resolutions are based on strengths.* I saw firsthand that these weren't just words. FGDM meant it.

As each participant was invited to share strengths (nothing was compulsory), I thought about all the difficulties and challenges that I had in my own life. In each and every instance, without exception, when I felt scared, confused, or angry, I reached for some inner strength that I possessed—some kind of skill, ability, knowledge, or faith—to tackle and overcome my life challenges. So, taking time to have the family members acknowledge their own and each other's strengths was much, much more than a mere "warm and fuzzy moment." It was absolutely necessary to the design and success of FGDM! It established an important and integral foundation and springboard from which to tackle the concerns that would follow. The logic and underlying value of using our strengths to help us resolve and solve our concerns, which in this case was child welfare but could be anything, was now for me fully, brilliantly illuminated and indelibly imprinted on my mind.

I was also awed as I watched the facilitator ask the family's permission to enforce the guidelines, one of which was "no shaming and blaming." It was here that I first witnessed the incredible art of strength-based work. If a family member or agency representative said something while sharing concerns that was clearly shaming or blaming (which was quite often the case), the facilitator politely and quickly interrupted that person and helped them reframe it into a strength-based statement.

An example: A family member pointed at another family member sitting across from her and said passionately and in a raised voice, "She can't take care of her kids. She has a drinking problem. She's the reason we're all here and why the kids are so fucked up." The facilitator responded, "I'm sorry. I need to interrupt you. I know we're all trying our best not to shame and blame. Let me see if I can help here. So are you saying that whoever the suggested caretaker is going to be for the children, you want to make sure that they don't have active alcohol issues because that may harm the children? That whoever all of you choose to take care of the kids, it's important that that person is clean and sober? Have I captured your concern?"

Then the facilitator said, "Remember, when you're thinking of a concern you want to share that focuses on your purpose and goal for your family conference, try and think about the issues underneath the concern. Without mentioning names or specific examples, what are the issues that you're thinking about? That address the child at risk and the welfare issues that all of you can and want to share, discuss, and help resolve? We can all talk about shared concerns, but shaming and blaming only leads to power struggles and fighting, and the kids end up being the losers."

The art of respectfully helping others to conceptualize and reframe in a strength-based manner—to help prevent that tangential arguing, mudslinging, shaming, and blaming that occurs when dealing with emotionally charged families, and which only serves to distract from the focus of child welfare and family stability—was and remains one of the most important lessons I've learned in my career thus far.

Perhaps the most extraordinary part of this conference, the part which was to set the tone for the rest of the time that I was allowed and privileged to be an FGDM practitioner, was the family alone time. Giving the family members an opportunity to freely, privately, and thoughtfully discuss all concerns shared thus far, while putting special emphasis on solving the focused goal laid out in the family-crafted purpose statement, was unheard of in our DCFS culture. DCFS actually leaving the room and essentially giving up its power to the family to design its own plan to address the child-welfare issues just wasn't done, mainly because its workers had always been professionally and interpersonally blinded by a deficit mind-set: *I'm the social worker, and I know what's wrong with you, and I know what you must do now, or else.*

Before the family alone time, the facilitator provided a simple matrix and one last respectful reminder to the family members that they were creating an action plan with action steps.

When the family had concluded its alone time and all participants had returned to the conference, the family presented a plan that was absolutely unbelievable.

I was happily shocked. The family plan specifically and comprehensively addressed the goals in the family-crafted purpose statement. It laid out what the parents had to do and by when, and declared that if they didn't meet their own agreed-to timetable and conditions—that is, if the parents "didn't get their act together," in the family's words—the children would be placed with a different family member.

Wow! This family plan asked the parents to do things that the agency never would have asked. The plan was more demanding on the family members than I think the agency would have been on them. I had always wondered why DCFS hadn't been giving the responsibility (read: power) to our families to create their own case plans. One can't empower unless one is willing to give up power.

As I watched and listened to the facilitator read the family plan aloud to the agency representative in front of everyone and then respectfully ask for the social worker's agreement and approval, I could see the family members' newfound pride and solidarity. At the beginning, the family members were pissed off at one another and it appeared as though it would be impossible to get them to agree on what day it was, let alone craft a complex, viable plan that solidly addressed all child-welfare issues. Now here they were, their facial expressions and body language clearly showing how proud they were of what they had accomplished. It was clear that the plan was *their plan*, a plan that they had voluntarily chosen, that made sense to them, that was aligned with their cultural values that allowed them to pick their own community-support resources. This process allowed this family and their friends to rise to the occasion and police their own, to hold their own accountable for their children. It worked big time!

The social worker couldn't believe her eyes and initially didn't know how to respond or what to say. When she found her bearings and words, she congratulated and thanked the family for its hard work and obvious love for its children. After a little negotiation on a couple details, she did agree to and approve the family plan. At the moment of the agreement, the facilitator turned again to the family and asked, "Can I get a round of applause for your hard work and this great plan?" The room broke out in pride-filled smiles and applause.

I had chills at this point. I was no longer holding on to one Social Work Moment last breath, I was now breathing freely and fully. What the family created with its plan, and the way it happened through this FGDM family conference model, embodied every great social work value and principle that we social workers are struggling for, fighting for, waiting to discover, and hoping to find before we take our collective last Social Work Moment breath. I was gratefully hooked and sold. I found my social worker home, FGDM.

I could share literally hundreds upon hundreds of FGDM family conferences, but three in particular stand out. These illustrate and highlight the profound potential and actual benefit of the social work tool, philosophy, and practice known as FGDM.

Ellis Island

When I was coordinating this conference, I ensured that the

biological mother, biological father, son, foster parent, case-carrying CSW, two rabbis, and a family friend attended.

I asked the mother, father, and son, who was in placement with a foster family, where they would like to have their conference. They said that they wanted to have it at their synagogue and that I needed to call their senior rabbi, which I did, asking his permission and explaining what the family conference was and how it worked.

When I mentioned that we would provide a light meal because the average family conference lasts four hours, the rabbi said, "Well, we have very specific requirements for any food served in our synagogue." As it turned out, I needed to follow several rules regarding kosher food. The rabbi was very gracious and shared that he was worried about and cared deeply for this family.

When all the participants were sitting around the table in the chairs that we had arranged, I realized that I was right in the middle of Ellis Island. I asked the family if it would like to begin its family conference with a traditional family opening. They, like many, started with a prayer, which the mother requested the senior rabbi give. Then the father said a short prayer, but he said it in a language that I didn't understand. Then the mother said a short prayer in Spanish, of which I only knew a little, and the junior rabbi finished with a few words, but again in a different language.

As it turned out, the mother was Latin and spoke a little Farsi and a little English but preferred Spanish. The father, who spoke very little English and Spanish and preferred Farsi, was Persian by birth and had converted. Their son grew up in the US and spoke little Farsi and some broken Spanish but preferred English. The senior rabbi spoke English, no Spanish, and some Farsi, but preferred Hebrew. The social worker was Caucasian and spoke only English. And to top it off, the foster parent was African American and didn't speak any Spanish, Farsi, or Hebrew, only English.

I had to quickly come up with a communication method so that all participants could communicate in a way that was most comfortable for them. My saving grace was the junior rabbi. Thank goodness, he spoke Farsi, Hebrew, English, and some Spanish. So I asked this junior rabbi to translate, and he graciously accepted. He helped translate the entire conference. It was fascinating and incredible to hear and experience all these languages and cultures come alive as these family and community participants struggled with the very challenging child-welfare topics and cultural diversities.

I've never forgotten how angrily and passionately the father spoke about his feelings and how, on several occasions, he directed his anger and cutting remarks at the mother. Several times I had to quickly insert myself, as the facilitator, to prevent shaming and blaming and do strength-based reframing. The reason I won't forget this wasn't because of the passionate feelings and often rage-filled words that the conference participants directed at one another. That was very commonplace, given the central theme of child removal and whether or not to return the child. The reason I won't forget is because of what happened when the rabbi spoke. The father, mother, and child became instantly contrite, still, and silent. It was very obvious that despite the tremendous cultural divergence within this family system, there was a common ground: clear respect for the religious leader. When the rabbi spoke, this entire family listened. No court, social worker, outside authority, agency, or non-family person could have done what this rabbi did when he spoke. They didn't have to listen; *they chose to.*

Families in the system need an opportunity to gather in their own homes, neighborhoods, churches, parks, and other familiar places so that they can police and hold their own accountable with the support of their blood relatives, religious leaders, family friends, and children.

"Ellis Island" ran much longer than the average family conference, but it was so worth it. Like hundreds of times before and since, the family came up with a great, practical, and viable family plan. The social worker was very impressed with how this conference model respectfully, seamlessly, and effectively handled all the cultural diversity issues.

I now say that I've been to Ellis Island twice. The first time was as part of FGDM.

The Hatfields and McCoys Circle Up

I coordinated a family conference that included several extended maternal and paternal family members as well as both biological parents. As I called every potential and actual participant who was going to attend the conference, it became very clear that there was a river of bad blood between the maternal and paternal sides of this family, which was a very common occurrence.

As I talked to one family member after another, I kept hearing how one side didn't trust the other side. I kept hearing how each side felt that the other side really didn't love the kids; that they had some ulterior motive; that they really didn't care about what was happening to the children.

One of the important jobs of an FGDM coordinator or facilitator was to "shake the bushes," as we used to say. It meant to reach out to anyone and everyone who truly loved the children and cared about their future welfare. FGDMs philosophy was that the greater number of family members that gathered and mobilized, that better chance they had of building a viable, stable, and long-term safety net for the children.

In cases with feuding families, the often herculean challenge was convincing the would-be participants that it was imperative to invite everyone who loved the children for the children's sake. We would tell them that we understood it might not be easy to sit across from family members about whom they held such strong negative feelings. We understood that there was a great deal of bad blood, but we would have guidelines at the conference and a very well-trained facilitator who would make sure the focus and goal would always be the best interest of the children. Shaming and blaming would be politely and quickly redirected, without exception, because the children were counting on all of us. We essentially guaranteed to all participants that their conference would not turn into a dogfight and mudslinging session, and their absence would diminish the potential benefit to the children. And we meant every single word.

With the family's agreement, I selected a conference room at the local city cultural center. But we quickly changed location when some family members told us that most of the family was headed to a different venue, the result of a communication break-down. I was waiting at the center when some of the family members came in and introduced themselves. They said that many other family members had been told to go to one of our local offices. The family members who came to the cultural center made one last attempt to exclude the other side, but I again repeated all that I had told them on the phone. Some of these family members said they couldn't guarantee that they would participate, to which I told them that I of course would honor their decision because it was their family conference.

I arrived at the new site and set up. At the last minute, I was fortunate to reach the paternal side's pastor, who told me he was well aware and well informed about the intense animosity and distrust between many of the family members. Still, he agreed to come.

Everyone showed. It was easy to pick out the two sides by where each sat. Again, this was very commonplace and it is very human for family members to pick a side.

As always, I began by asking the family how to start its

conference. They unsurprisingly chose to open with a prayer. Both sides chose the paternal side's pastor to say the prayer, which was a surprise and a good omen. Was I glad he was there.

For the vast majority of families, the time to share strengths is the first time the kids hear the grown-ups say anything vaguely nice about one another. They hear such strengths as "She's very caring," "He works very hard to provide," "She's a good listener," "She's always been there for the kids," "Tommy is very good at sports," "He has a great relationship with the children," "She's always helped them with their homework," "He loves the children." It's a powerful moment for the kids.

What's also very fascinating and rarely considered is that an FGDM conference is often the first time that so many of a family's members have sat down together in years, or ever. What seems to happen is that the issues that bring the nuclear family to DCFS's attention also seem to create deep and seemingly impassable divisions in these family systems. Add to this dynamic the extensive lack of actual facts and substitute them with hearsay, gossip, and conjecture, and you have the perfect breeding ground for the Hatfields and the McCoys. *We hate them and don't trust them just because.*

Feuding families typically share strengths only about their side. I expected this to happen here, but something changed. One of the children, a bright twelve-year-old girl, wanted to share some strengths. She was enjoying seeing and being around all her family members, some of whom she had only heard about or seen in an occasional picture. She started by saying that she liked how her paternal uncle was always so nice to her and that she loved him for it. Then she said that her maternal grandmother was a good cook and she loved to eat her food. But what she said last—I don't mind saying because it has happened many times before— choked me up and made my eyes misty. She said, "I love all my family and need to see all my family."

All the adult family members sat silently for what seemed like an eternity but was probably only a minute or so. Then the father, who had sounded and seemed the angriest at the maternal side, spoke up. He said that he wanted to say that he did appreciate how well the maternal grandmother was taking care of his children, and with a wry smile added, "Yeah, she is a good cook." The children had been removed from the father and mother and placed with the maternal grandmother. For the father to make this concession, prompted by his daughter, was huge.

But then it came time to share concerns that specifically addressed their agreed-to purpose statement: "For the family to decide where the children were going to continue to live that will meet all their needs, and how the entire family can work together to support the parents."

The brief and fleeting moments of peace and detente quickly deteriorated into World War III. I definitely earned my facilitator title that night. It was rapid-fire shaming and blaming. I was interrupting and reframing, it seemed, almost every other participant. The father was again furious and the mother equally so. If looks and glares could kill, many would have either died or been arrested that night. Both sides again seemed to pick battle lines and hunker down for a long fight.

Now came time for the family to be alone. The family agreed to allow one non-family member, the pastor, to stay. I asked for two volunteers on both sides of the family to enforce the family guidelines, especially the "no shaming and blaming" one, but I didn't hold out much hope that they would succeed.

As I walked out of the room, I told the family that I would not return until they called me back, so that they knew that their time would be private and undisturbed. It was very common during this alone time for families to experience what we called a "storming period." During this period, many of our families would invariably vent any and all emotions with and, in many cases, at each other. We would hear shouting, name-calling, and very emotionally charged verbiage coming from the sequestered family members. But as it happened so many, many times before, once they got past all the venting of raw emotions, they somehow chose to get something accomplished, and with very, very few exceptions, found a way to come up with a viable family plan.

I was very worried that this might end up being one of those rare exceptions where the raw hurt and pain between these family members would prevent them from elevating their obvious love for the children above their anger, hurt, and distrust for one another. I was already preparing my "you gave it a good try" speech.

Half an hour passed by and I, unable to help myself, carefully and quietly walked over to the door. I could hear quiet voices. I wasn't sure in which direction things were moving. An hour passed by and they were still in there. Could it be?

Then I heard shouting again for about five minutes. Then it got silent. Another half hour passed, and my cell phone rang. I was about as nervous and anxious as I had ever been. I had no idea what to expect.

I walked into the room and couldn't believe my eyes. They were all holding hands in a circle, maternal and paternal family members intermingled. I definitely got more than a little misty then, but I didn't care. They had elected the pastor to read their family plan. Included in it was a unanimous agreement for the entire family to start having everyone gather in one place so that they could start to get to know each other. But the maternal grandmother had to be in charge of cooking.

I wish I had the ability to put into words just how I felt. The words that come closest are: "transformational," "magical," and "damn grateful for having the privilege to be a witness." This family freely found its way and chose to disarm and surrender its weapons of rage and distrust and instead build an unselfish and loving circle of support for and around the children.

Mommy's Love

I thought that this one was going to be pretty straightforward. All the family members I could reach were pretty supportive of the mother getting her child back. The child had been placed in a paternal relative's home. Both sides shared concerns about the mother possibly relapsing. Apparently, the mother had a long history of alcoholism, but now, after a great deal of reported hard work and the successful completion of a drug program, she was clean and sober. Even when the family members shared concerns about a relapse, they all quickly followed their comments with a quick, "But she is doing great and deserves to have her child back. They need each other," or "She has worked her ass off. She did what she needed to do." All the family members seemed to know and like each other. They were unanimous in their motivation to see mother and child reunited.

I arrived an hour early, as I usually did, to set up and get a sense of the environment. I used a local office that was central to all the participants. I always made my best effort to conduct the conference wherever the family was comfortable, so I've used the family home, a park, a community center, a church, a public library, a synagogue, the back of my car in a parking lot (a long story), a sheriff's station, out of state, a private office, and our office, among other places. I always remembered that it was their family conference, and I was their guest.

As the participants arrived, most of them came up to the mother and shared words of support and encouragement to her about getting her child back. During the strength-sharing phase, every participant shared great, glowing strengths about each other, and most made sure to say something especially supportive and reaffirming of the mother.

I thought, *Boy, this is going to be quick and painless. Great! I was due for an easy one.* It came time to have the participants share their concerns that specifically addressed their agreed-to family purpose statement: "For the family to come up with a plan for the child to return to the home and care of her mother, that would meet all her needs and keep her safe, with strong support for the mother."

The family members shared concerns that were very thoughtful and took into consideration the need to help the mother develop a commonsense and viable relapse-prevention strategy for her alcoholism. I thought, *I wish I could videotape this conference to show other families just how maternal and paternal sides can work together.*

The mother was one of the last adults to share her concerns. She shared statements that highlighted the work and commitment necessary to establish her newfound clean-and-sober lifestyle and status. She thanked the relatives who had and were taking care of her daughter. As she talked, her voice began to crack, and she teared up. All the participants appeared very sympathetic and, in many cases, empathic with what this mother had gone through to fight her way back.

The social worker's job was to share the agency's child safety and at-risk issues. This was usually moderately to significantly challenging for the social worker. Many of my colleagues still operated under a deficit framework. They saw and related to our families through their reported and recorded deficits. So my fellow social workers would share concerns such as, "You need to attend AA classes," "You need to agree to more drug testing," and "Since you have a history of alcoholism . . ."

When this happened, I quickly intervened and helped out my well-intentioned colleagues. I would say, "Instead of listing what you think this family should or should not do, which is highly disrespectful, especially when in someone else's home, it may be more helpful for you as a representative of your agency to share what the underlying concerns are, and then allow the family in the private alone time to determine how they feel and what they believe is the best way to address all concerns, including your agency's concerns. So, for instance, regarding substance-abuse issues, try saying something like, 'Our agency wants to make sure that whoever the caregiver is going to be, that person is drug- and alcohol-free,' or "Whomever this family picks to be the primary caregiver, they must be clean and sober.'"

I almost always privately shared a few hints to help the social worker recognize when they may be unintentionally shaming and blaming. I let them know that any time they started a sentence with "you" when sharing concerns, it almost always lead to shaming and blaming. Also, it was a good idea to always avoid stating someone's name or a specific example (which the family already knew, as they would always know much more then we would or should ever know) because it would almost always lead to shaming and blaming, which would only lead to people becoming defensive, shutting down, or becoming adversarial.

This social worker did exceptionally well. She was very impressed with this family, and it was easy to see that she was a huge advocate for the mother. She made sure to say, at least three times, that she admired the mother's efforts and hard work, and that it was clear that the mother loved her daughter. It again looked like this was going to be a pretty cut-and-dried family conference with everyone in full agreement.

Before moving into family alone time, I remembered to ask the child if she wanted to share some concerns. Including the child and giving him or her a voice was absolutely central to FGDM. In fact, it might have been the only time that the child felt included and was literally given a voice, resulting in him or her feeling empowered.

Unless it was unquestionably obvious that the child felt comfortable and safe, I always walked out of the room and privately asked the child if he or she wanted to share some concerns. It was important to remember just how intimidating sharing concerns was for a child with a group of old farts, be they parents, close relatives, or others.

So I was outside with this girl and I asked her if she understood what was happening and if she wanted to share anything. She made it clear that she understood. Then she paused and lowered her head to where I couldn't see her eyes. I gave her all the time she needed. After about a minute or so, she raised her head and looked at me with a thoughtful and concerned face. She asked, "Is it okay for me to say anything?" I told her it was and added, "It will help all your family in there to make the best decisions for you if they hear everything you want to say."

A child's choice of words in this context can be very challenging. On one hand, you want them to know that what they have to say is very important, but, on the other hand, you don't want them to feel pressured into having to say something that they may later regret for reasons that you may not fully understand or appreciate. Striking the right balance and tone is part of the art of being a FGDM facilitator.

I asked her if she wanted to tell me her concerns in private so I could write them down and then go back in and read them to her family; this I did quite often with kids. She thought long and hard about it and then said with confidence in her voice, "No, I want to say them."

I told her that it might help to pick out a person with whom she felt comfortable and look at that person while she talked. I also told her that I had a secret word that I sometimes used with kids. This was a word that, if the child said it because it was getting too hard to finish sharing their concerns, I would quickly take over and make sure they were okay. I told her the word: "tired." She smiled and took a deep breath, and in we walked. I knew she was going to be okay. I announced to the group that she wanted to share her concerns. I also reminded the group to remember that this wasn't easy for children.

She started by saying that she worried about her mom

hurting herself, speaking about her in the second person as kids usually did. She said that she cried herself to sleep many nights, wishing and praying for her mother to stop drinking. Her mother started tearing up, but it was clear that she didn't want to interrupt her daughter or cause her to stop. The girl said that she was happy to hear that her mother had stopped drinking and that she wanted to believe it. Then she made one last statement: "I was so afraid when she drank and she would get so angry . . ." Her voice started to crack and her eyes teared up. Then she said "tired" and I stepped in.

The family was about to move into its alone time. I had no doubt that the plan was going to be great and that the social worker, who was obviously very supportive of the mother reuniting with her daughter, would enthusiastically agree to and approve it. Having a family and our agency agree so easily was no easy task for a myriad of complex and serious reasons. But we seemed to have it here.

As I excused the family into alone time, the mother spoke up and asked if she could share one last concern that she hadn't been able to before. I said of course.

She stood up and said to her daughter with pain and hurt in her eyes, "I'm sorry that Mommy scared you those times when I drank. That was wrong of Mommy. Mommy wasn't being honest with you or herself. I'm so scared of losing you. That hurts Mommy more than anything." Tears fell and her voice cracked and faded but still was audible. I kept one eye on her daughter and listened for the word "tired," just in case she found the moment too much. The mother paused, lowered her head slightly, and closed her eyes, still shedding tears for what felt like a long time. Finally, the mother clenched her fists, straightened her body as if she was trying to gather her strength, raised her head, and opened her eyes. She spoke again, saying, "Sweetheart, I love you so much. Mommy doesn't want to lie to you anymore, Mommy doesn't ever want to make you afraid again, I'm so sorry I did that. Mommy isn't ready for you to come home yet. This is so hard for me to say, I need more time. I want you to come home when you'll never, ever have to leave Mommy again. I love you."

The family decided to keep the child were she was. The mother stated that she would enroll in a drug and alcohol inpatient program. I later learned that she did that and eventually reunited with her daughter.

If we social workers and agencies do our job right and give our families genuine and heartfelt respect, support, and trust, and if we give up some power to empower our families, who knows what can happen. If we can give our families an honest opportunity to take care of their own, maybe we'll hear about or be really lucky to witness one our kids experiencing a mother's love.

The Family Group Decision Making (FGDM) program existed for approximately eight years, during which time it touched and transformed the lives of countless families. For those many, it was a turning point that gave them an opportunity to chart their own course, to find their way back to providing for their family, to establish or reestablish their family unity, to instill or re-instill feelings of safety and genuine and unselfish concern, and to have their family once again, or maybe for the first time, feel loved by their own.

Unfortunately, because of reasons such as staffing constraints, economics, politics, and the intrinsic fear that bureaucracies seem to have regarding giving up power, countless more families never had their FGDM family conference.

Change, to most bureaucracies, especially one as gargantuan as ours, doesn't come easily or quickly. A recent director (they don't seem to stick around very long) once told me, "In my tenure, I'll realistically have a chance to get about three things done, to make three changes. That's all." There seems to be some omnipotent and omnipresent force whose only purpose is to maintain the status quo at all costs—and I mean *at all costs*—even when DCFS knows that a program works and is the right thing to do, and when that program has had a successful eight-year run and has been backed by a commissioned study by an independent, credible research team that concluded that the overwhelming majority of our families had been helped.

Many can and probably always will speculate as to why this program that definitively and positively touched so many lives was terminated. My guess is that when the department found itself with a backlog of between thirty to forty thousand calls to emergency child abuse hotlines that needed to be investigated, Los Angeles County decided it needed the FGDM people working on that. Plus, not everyone liked or believed in empowering families.

Still, no one can deny that our case families had received an honest opportunity to love, care, and stand up for their own, and were treated by FGDM practitioners with respect, support, and cultural sensitivity.

FGDM indeed was an improbable course correction, but from the very beginning, we worked hard at winning over our DCFS culture. A former FGDM manager used to remind us over and over, "This won't be easy, we're going to run into a lot of resistance. Just trust the model and its values. We will win their hearts and minds."

In the beginning we constantly heard: "The conferences are too long," "What do you mean leave families alone to make their own plans? They've already fucked up their lives," "Why are you wasting time with talking about strengths? Do you know what they did?" "What do you mean give them back some power?" "I'm not going to their house," "You can't trust them, they lie," and "They need to do what I'm telling them to do."

Despite all this, FGDM overcame this bias, prejudice, intolerance, and fear. We did for a time win over our DCFS culture, and FGDM, which seemed as surreal as that fabled creature the unicorn, came to life and was real. We used it to do real social work, and we helped families. We had the privilege of respectfully entering our families' lives as genuine, non-adversarial community helpers, to do what social work was always meant to do.

We empowered families and gave them hope.

A Second Time We Got It Right

I was perhaps more fortunate than most, though some of it probably was just dumb luck. I was already in a new, innovative, and incredible program, FGDM. FGDM had such a great collection of social worker values and principles, including treating families with unconditional respect, looking at and working with families based on their strengths, and empowering families to make and own their decisions and choices. All these great values and principles were based on the families' culturally driven values and beliefs, with sound but non-adversarial checks and balances.

I had been working in this program for about two years when it occurred to me that I could take these great FGDM values and principles and apply them to another population that sorely needed them and was dramatically underserved: our transitional youth population.

Historically, the statistics have been and continue to be very bleak for our youths who age out of the system, usually around their eighteenth birthday. By "aging out," I'm referring to our youths who have their dependency case terminated by dependency court, which means that they're on their own. While our dependency court and social workers make a collective and concerted effort to help our transitional youths gain the tools they need to make it on their own, most, tragically, don't and won't.

Statistics tell us that, year after year, the vast majority of our transitional youths who age out end up homeless, jobless, incarcerated, and with inflamed mental-health issues. Many have never had even one single dependable, healthy, adult relationship. Many also end up having children out of wedlock and contracting STDs. It's not a pretty or hopeful picture. I'm sure it's one of the reasons why we see so many of our transitional kids sabotage their emancipation as they get closer and closer to finishing their high school requirements and to their eighteenth birthdays, the two principal benchmarks for our dependency court when deciding to "JT" (Jurisdiction Terminated) our transitional kids.

While attending an FGDM international conference, I had the good fortune to attend a workshop where an FGDM practitioner had used the FGDM principles and some of its format to create a conference experience for transitional youths. I was fascinated and intrigued, knowing the desperate needs of DCFS transitional youth. Sitting next to me at that workshop was my FGDM manager, who could see my excitement by my squirming. She looked at me, smiled, and, without even asking what I was thinking because she could see it in my eyes, said, "Go for it!"

One of the major issues that needed to be addressed was that most of our kids didn't see their leaving the system as a spring-board to a happy, exciting, and prosperous future. For many and probably most, the word "emancipation" conjured up visions of a cold and uncaring cliff, and when they dared to peer over the edge, they saw an abyss, isolating and unknown. And it scared the hell out of them.

Before I designed my model, I had decided on a name: Emancipation Conference (E-conf). I wanted to make sure that I could do a good job of helping mitigate the understandable and intense fear that our kids have regarding emancipation, and find a way to supplant the fear with knowledge. For most of us, there are few things in this world more terrifying then the unknown. Pretend for a moment that you have no family and no real friends, and while there are some people trying to meet some of your needs, you feel that you don't know or are connected to anyone who really, really knows you and loves you unconditionally. Add to this scenario the fact that the few individuals who have been meeting some of your basic needs (food, clothing, medical care, and shelter) are now going away on your eighteenth birthday. Can anyone, even for a split second, imagine what the unknown means to that young person? Most of us, myself included, don't want to go there.

I started to think back to when I was a transitional youth. Felt like a hundred years ago. What could have helped me, what would have taken away some of that fear? I also began thinking about my sons, who were in transition at the time. And, most importantly, I spent much time trying to recall the transitional kids I had worked with. I asked myself, "Why have transitional kids come to me? How was I able to help them?" A light bulb went on. Facts! Transitional youths, including my own sons, wanted to know the facts and how to access them. They wanted to know where to go, who to call, and what is out there that could really help them.

Thus was born the resource binder. This binder grew into a comprehensive collection of tangible, viable, and current resources and information that the youths could use in real time or simply refer to at any point along their emancipation journey. It had four principal sections: transitional housing, education, vocation, and Independent Transitional Living (a DCFS internal program). This resource binder soon became one of the Emancipation Conference's most sought-after by-products. Everybody wanted it: the transitional youth's social worker; the foster parent, caregiver, or legal guardian; and community agency partners.

Our children's social workers (CSWs), who care deeply about the kids, simply didn't and don't have the time to stay current on what viable resources are available to our transitional kids. Most CSWs simply didn't and don't know enough about how to help transitional dependents of the court navigate the educational, financial aid, and transitional housing systems. They simply didn't and don't have the time or energy given their overwhelming caseloads. Add to this the fact that our CSW demographic seemed to be getting younger and younger, and many CSWs were having their own informal experience with emancipation. But after these youths leave the system, they aren't thought about much.

I've always been puzzled and deeply disturbed that the department has never demonstratively prioritized this population. Case in point: DCFS has a position called an Independent Living Program Coordinator (ILPC). This person's main job is to help transitional youths understand and use the DCFS Independent Living Program, which was created to help the kids successfully emancipate, or at least have a better shot at it. Each office has an ILPC that is responsible for covering anywhere from about five hundred to more than seven hundred kids. Put this into perspective. The average CSW's caseload includes between thirty and forty-five kids. Tragically according to multiple independent audits like SB (senate bill) 2030; Child Welfare Services Workload Study - Final Report, April 2000: CSW's are only supposed to have case loads of about 15 kids for Family Maintenance/ Reunification; and about 13 kids for Emergency Response case loads, to have any chance at being effective and helping to keep kids safe; still waiting for this to happen. Many of the focus group participants expressed concern that due to inadequate time, support, and resources, staff members are burning out.

Now consider that an ILPC is responsible for between five hundred to seven hundred transitional youths, who constitute unequivocally one of the most challenging, complex, and time-consuming populations. And the overwhelming majority of ILPCs care very deeply about our kids, and have made a huge difference for the kids that they were able reach and help. But could you handle five to seven hundred by yourself? Furthermore, that ILPC is a supervisor without underlings; he or she is flying solo. For many of us, the ILPC position has been and continues to appear, sadly and tragically, to be only "window dressing" and little more.

In creating my Emancipation Conference, I began thinking about how I could adapt what I learned from the FGDM workshop, keeping in mind the service needs of our transitional kids. I spent a great deal of time working on an agenda model and format that would meaningfully address every issue possible while ensuring that I never strayed from my FGDM values and principles.

I made sure to remember the developmental age and culture of transitional teens. One such truth: you don't tell a teen what to do. Teens are trying to define themselves, develop belief and value systems, and build confidence in their own judgment. I knew it was most important that they trust themselves to navigate their world, as, for the most part, they were cut off from their families of origin and the accompanying human connections and support.

So I wanted to make certain my E-conference agenda and structure were designed to empower our kids rather than dictate to them what they should do. I wanted an agenda that was developmentally sensitive and culturally respectful, that invited our youths to be in absolute control of their choices and decisions and, most importantly, the plan that resulted from the E-conf. It had to be a plan created by the transitional youth, along with the adult and other supports at the conference, and be focused on their concerns, fears, wishes, goals, and hopes.

I also wanted to completely change the way DCFS frames emancipation. Too often and for far too long, emancipation has been seen and articulated by social workers and the courts as an event. When you turn eighteen and graduate, "You're on your own, kid." How incredibly absurd, insane, and counterintuitive this is. Having worked and volunteered with the transitional population for some thirty years, I never have met a youth who was ready to make it on his or her own on his or her eighteenth birthday, including my own sons.

My E-conf agenda needed to ensure and make abundantly clear that emancipation is a *process* and not an event. This was, from all the discussions that I have had with countless transitional kids over the years, a huge part of the incredible fear that they form around emancipating from the system.

I thought long and hard about feeling alone and isolated, because the kids struggle with it. I thought about what would have happened if my own sons hadn't been able to call me for support during their transitions. Fortunately, they had been, and the reality is that transition is a lifelong process and journey. I don't want to think of what would have or could have happened if I wasn't around to support them, guide them, or listen to them when they were confused, afraid, unsure, happy, or excited and just wanting to share it with someone who really knew them and really cared—with someone who loved them.

My E-conf agenda and structure needed to be as inclusive as possible. I needed to make sure that we took the necessary time to "shake the bushes" and find every important person in the transitional youth's life that really knew and cared about them. And it needed the people from whom the transitional youth felt love and support, no matter how small that number was.

Another issue that I needed to consider was the "old fart dilemma." This piggybacked on the developmental level of this transitional population. I knew from extensive experience with my DCFS cohorts what would happen when you get a kid in a room with a group of older helping professionals. You would have these well-meaning CSWs preaching to the kid and telling him or her what to do, how they're screwing up, and what should be their priorities.

The vast majority of these old or older farts are very well-intentioned and doing what comes naturally and normally to them, given their developmental level, and they're doing it because they care. Like me, they want to give back and pass on.

But they might not realize that our transitional youths need our support to help them believe in themselves, and so they might have to do what may feel so unnatural to us.

So to mitigate this potential derailing, I borrowed the FGDM family conference guidelines, which essentially ask the conference attendees permission to enforce the conference rules in support of the family, in this case the transitional youth. Now I had something to keep all well-meaning adults in check, myself included.

The following agenda and suggested guidelines became the emancipation conference agenda for almost seven years, before it met its untimely, tragic, still-puzzling, and sudden demise:

Guidelines

Focus on the Purpose: Support of the emancipation plan's success

Encourage Honesty: Respect the transitioning youth's best interest and emancipation wishes

Everyone is Important: Each person speaks in turn, one at a time

Respect: Everyone is entitled to give and receive it

Listen: Hear and support the transitioning youth's goals

Permission: To enforce these guidelines

Agenda

I.   **Opening:** Welcome, invitation of family tradition, self-introductions, and explanation of rules/guidelines

II.   **Three Phases:** Strengths, goals, needs

    A.   **Strengths**

    B.   **Goals:** Short-term (next twelve months) and long-term (two to four years)

       1. Education

      2. Vocation

      3. Personal

    C. **Needs:** Short-term (next twelve months) and long-term (two to four years)

      1. Education

      2. Vocation

      3. Personal

III. **Emancipation Options**

    A. Housing

    B. School

    C. Employment

IV. **Necessary Emancipation Documents**

V. **Miscellaneous:** Issues not yet addressed

VI. **Circle of Support:** Pre- and post-emancipation

VII. **Emancipation Action Grid:** Covers housing, employment, education, finances, transportation, personal care, medical and dental, necessary emancipation documents, and desired emancipation day

    A. Things to do

    B. By whom

    C. Date to be completed

For years, the emancipation conferences of countless transitional youths and young adults tangibly and concretely helped them. Foster parents were so grateful to have the resource binder, which brought them so much great information. I had so many foster parents ask, "Can I have one for my other kids in my house?" "Can I have one to just put on my coffee table?" I had so many social workers ask for a resource binder and thank me for making it. They would exclaim, "There's no way I could have the time to put all this great information together in one place."

I also initially never anticipated the E-conf becoming a critically important teaching and empowering tool not just for the transitional youth, but also for the youth's entire support group. The E-conf educated all attendees about all the available transitional resources for the kids. It also helped the youths feel not so alone. The E-conf gave the youths that rare opportunity to feel a sense of control over their lives at this critical transitional juncture. They crafted their plan with the support of the facilitator and attendees with whom they felt safe, who cared about them, and who genuinely wanted them to succeed. And only the youths could determine who came to their E-conf and who didn't—I made sure of it.

The E-conf provided the entire support group, including the caregiver and CSW, a chance to hear the youth detail his or her wishes, hopes, and short- and long-term educational, vocational, and personal goals. And every social worker who came to a youth's E-conf was given a resource binder.

The opening strength segment of the E-conf was especially powerful for a countless number of our kids. We would give all the attendees an opportunity to share the youth's strengths. I wish I could have videotaped these kids' faces as they sat and listened. For many of them, it could have been the first, only, and last time a group of people that they trusted publicly shared strengths such as, "He's really good at math," "She is great with kids," "He has an incredible voice," "She writes so beautifully," "Boy, he can take anything apart and put it back together again," and on and on. While they shared, the facilitator or co-facilitator wrote these shared strengths down on a big easel for everyone to see.

I can't count the times a youth came up to me during or after his or her conference and asked me, "Can I have that page, you know, the strength one?"

For a program, especially such a new program, to be accepted and have any shot at lasting in our DCFS world, it has to have broad acceptance and appeal among CSWs, administrators, and courts. For that to happen, it has to deliver the goods and help our clients, in this case our transitional youths. Within a very short period, E-confs did just that.

Our court would routinely order an E-conf. CSWs would routinely refer their transitional-aged kids to E-confs. I would get numerous E-conf requests from the community, various community-based agencies, and stakeholders that were also working with the kids.

The E-conf's universal and unanimous buy-in was predicated on one simple fact: it worked! CSWs now had a tool that really helped them help their transitional youths. The transitional youths now had an empowering experience from people who really listened to them, and they walked out with answers to the three most important transitional questions: "Who can I call?" "How do I do it?" and "Where do I go?" They would actually craft a concrete plan, their plan, which they could hold, look at, and reference. It was their road map to help them navigate their transitional process. It also provided support so that everyone concerned could help the transitional youth find his or her way to his or her goals and a successful emancipation.

The facilitator drafted a comprehensive summary after every E-conf. One of the last statements in the summary was a statement directed specifically at our dependency court. This was a summation statement letting the court know the transitional youth's perspective on when the youth felt ready to emancipate and under what conditions, the areas that the youth felt that he or she needed to complete, and resources (finances, housing, etc.) available so the youth could emancipate and have his or her case closed.

In our DCFS world, people think trying to implement a new program is like trying to change a tire on a moving car. Over the years, I have learned and personally experienced that the car is not only moving, but sometimes someone is also hitting your legs with a stick. Emancipation conferences were a very rare and happy exception to the rule.

E-confs ended after about seven years. Why? No one has ever officially explained why. My guess is that they ended for the same reason the FGDMs ended: At or around that time, DCFS needed all available personnel to tackle the mysterious backlog of thirty to forty thousand Emergency Response referrals. These are the Child Abuse Hotline referrals that are called in.

Since E-confs ended, nothing has been put in place to provide the kind of concrete, respectful, and targeted support that those three-hour E-confs provided, and nothing has matched its accomplishments. Nothing has even come vaguely close to helping us social workers help our transitional youths successfully emancipate.

Change is hard for most of us, but for bureaucracies, that difficulty is multiplied. For large and very large bureaucracies such as DCFS, change seems unachievable. For any success we achieve, the pendulum eventually swings back to old, familiar social-work practices: the ones that allow DCFS to maintain the highest degree of control and power. Sadly and tragically, our transitional kids remain profoundly underserved.

I don't know what it takes to make permanent, progressive change in the DCFS culture. I do know that we have a large body of great, compassionate, highly skilled, intelligent, and creative social workers, supervisors, and support staff who are waiting for the next chance to prioritize our transitional kids and help them have the best possible shot at successfully emancipating and making it on their own.

I have every confidence we still can, and must, do this.

Vicarious Traumatization and Self-Care

I decided one day that I wasn't going to just stand by and watch as this work caused another helping professional to crash and burn without doing something about it. These helping professionals were significantly diminished emotionally, spiritually, and physically, and, in many cases, damaged. They were, as a direct result of their work with their clients and case families, changed.

I'm not referring to the kind of positive change that we all hope to experience after giving so much of ourselves doing something as important as spending a career helping others. I'm speaking of the kind of change that comes from having your core beliefs assaulted day after day, week after week, and month after month, for year after year. It's the kind of change that leaves one asking when looking in the mirror at night, "Who am I?" or "What's happened to me?" or "What is happening to me?" or "Why am I doing this?" or "Is this what I wanted to do with my life?"

For more than twenty years, I personally witnessed people in my profession, as well as countless others in other helping professions, end up personally damaged by the work they were doing. Their core beliefs about themselves, others, and their worldview became dramatically skewed. Their work lives as helping professionals were causing tremendous disruption, pain, and confusion for their loved ones, who found themselves asking, "What's happening to you and to us? You're changing—you're not the same person anymore. Why?"

In short, their work in helping a traumatized population was invading and, in many, many cases, destroying their personal lives. Why?

I couldn't just stand by and watch anymore. I was determined to try and understand what was happening to me and my fellow helping professionals. And, more importantly, what could be done about it.

I started to research the issue and spent several years reading everything I could find. I discovered such terms as compassion fatigue, secondary stress, and secondary traumatic stress syndrome. These terms seemed to be the answer. They focused on the effects of work on the helping professional.

I thought, *This is great!* Finally, someone has given language and meaning to what was happening to helping professionals and the personal impact we experienced. These terms, as I discovered, primarily focused on a set of symptoms and common reactions that helping professionals across the wide spectrum of helping professions exhibited as they worked with people experiencing pain, loss, and trauma.

I found several studies that highlighted the tremendous burnout rate among helping professionals in fields such as social work, law enforcement, psychology, and clergy. There were several articles and books that focused on a set of symptoms that helping professionals often exhibit after working with a traumatized population.

Symptoms included hyper-vigilance, insomnia, hypersomnia, anxiety, avoidance behaviors, withdrawal, intrusive thoughts and or images, reliving perceived or experienced trauma, recurrent distressing dreams, acting or feeling as if the traumatic event were recurring, feeling of detachment, sense of a foreshortened future, difficulty with memory and concentration, etc.

While these terms, Secondary Traumatic Stress, Compassion Fatigue and Secondary Stress, seemed to explain some of what was going on with helping professionals, something was still missing. These terms primarily focused on the symptoms, which troubled me. They didn't seem to explain the profound change to the helping professional's self, specifically how the helping professional feels and believes about "others," "worldview," and "self."

These terms didn't explain the slow, pervasive, and discreet impact on our characters and personalities while working with a traumatized population. They didn't speak to the self that was clearly under assault and in countless instances changed somehow— disfigured and damaged by the very work itself. How and why?

I almost gave up hope of finding what I sought, thinking that maybe I or someone else would simply need to create a new term to capture what was and is happening to helping professionals. But I kept reading. I'm not sure how and when it happened, but somehow I stumbled onto some weird term called "vicarious traumatization." At first, I thought it sounded like psychobabble, that it was simply a new wrapper with the same meaning as the previous terms. I expected to read more of what I had already discovered about secondary trauma and compassion fatigue. I was happily wrong.

I was surprised yet eternally grateful to discover much, much more. This was really it! Vicarious traumatization (VT) was the construct that I had hoped to find. A therapist named Laurie Ann Pearlman and her colleague Karen Saakvitne coined the term. Pearlman had seen, over an extended period, a very clear pattern of reactions from the therapists who worked in her clinical psychotherapeutic practice.

Her therapists, as a direct result of working with their clients (the traumatized population), consistently and universally exhibited a number of symptoms that mimicked symptoms commonly found in such clinical disorders as post-traumatic stress disorder and depression. Some of these symptoms I mentioned above: hyper-vigilance, hyper-arousal, irritability, sleep disturbance, diminished empathy, and reliving trauma. But there was also a heightened startle response, depression, difficulty trusting, loss of energy, feelings of hopelessness, crying jags, and avoidance behaviors.

As Pearlman wrote in her book *Transforming the Pain,* "All of the trauma work that we do, hour after hour, day after day, week after week, contributes to inner changes in the self of the therapist. It's an inevitable part of the work . . . because we're entering into a very dark world, and if we're open emotionally, in the way we need to be to be effective helpers, we're going to be impacted."

I ordered and read everything I could from this author. Along with *Transforming the Pain,* I was fortunate enough to find a training video that provided the direct observations and data that she later used to create the construct known as vicarious traumatization (VT).

As I watched this video over and over and listened to this author and her therapists, it was uncanny how often their reactions and symptoms were identical to those experienced by me and all those social workers and helping professionals I had worked alongside or simply watched or heard about for years. We all struggled with the same reactions and issues. These people were being professionally affected but their impact was not just professional. It was clear that VT's effects were much more pervasive. It was invading their personal lives in significant and alarming ways.

The common denominator was the traumatized populations that we (Pearlman, her therapists, me, my fellow social workers) were trying to help. The other common thread was our empathic engagement.

The construct that Pearlman and Saakvitne created focuses on the slow, insidious buildup and assault on the core beliefs of helping professionals, namely how they feel and believe about others, themselves, and their worldviews. It focuses on how, over time, the self changes because of a constant assault on its core beliefs, and how those core beliefs become distorted as helping professionals work with a traumatized population for extended periods.

The assault on our core beliefs occurs when a helping professional works with a client and emphatically engages that client by caring, listening, and experiencing his or her reenactments of intense fear, sadness, anger, and, in many cases, rage. Simply put, helping professionals end up generating the same emotional reactions as our clients. This occurs even though we haven't personally experienced the trauma that our client shares with us. We, in essence, become indirectly traumatized. That is vicarious traumatization. So when helping professionals empathically engage client after client after client, over and over and over, for days, weeks, months, and, in some cases, years, we can and often find our core beliefs, our self, becoming significantly skewed, deformed, and changed. In countless cases, this assault, which occurs slowly and insidiously, damages countless helping professionals, including social workers.

The two most tragic and salient casualties of VT, corroborated by my professional and personal experience and a growing body of research, is the ability of helping professionals for empathy and trust. Our capacity to trust can and often does become diminished and sometimes simply disappears. One student in one of my trainings once remarked, "When I started, I wasn't that trusting, but now, I don't trust anyone, even my own father, and he's a good man."

One couple that was in a VT training session shared the following story: "We were at Disneyland, we had our four-and-a-half-year-old with us. Some park employee came up to us dressed as the character Goofy. My husband's first thought was, *What does he want with my son, why is he trying to shake his hand? What does he really want?"*

Our capacity for empathy also starts to fade. We become less able to separate our encounters with traumatized clients from contacts with other humans, including our loved ones. Our sense of safety and potential victimization becomes distorted. Many of us have awakened on some random normal day and realized that the core beliefs that use to define us have changed. We stare in the bathroom mirrors at the strained, puzzled, worried-stricken reflections and ask ourselves, "Who am I now?" and "What happened to me?"

It was time to do something. I took all that I had read, with special focus on VT, and I created a curriculum and training using VT as the principal construct to help social workers understand the profound impact on the self as they walked in that dark place with their traumatized population.

As I gave training after training, first starting with small focus groups, the reaction was incredible. I heard the same responses and saw the same reactions over and over from the participants, my colleagues.

I heard colleague after colleague say, "I'm not the same person anymore," "I just don't feel the same way about so many things," "My friends and family even say, 'You're different now,'" "I look in the mirror and I'm not sure I recognize me anymore. It scares and saddens me," "I feel like I'm the one who's been traumatized," "I just want it to stop, to end," "I don't know if I can make it," "I've just stopped trusting people," "I don't even want to be around people anymore, I was never like this before," "I don't trust anyone now," "I feel so alone."

I've amassed hundreds of anonymous VT training surveys from social workers, probation officers, therapists, teachers, attorneys, child-welfare group home staff, court-assigned special advocate (CASA) workers, and other helping professionals. When they first returned these surveys, I thought it was a mere coincidence that their comments and responses were virtually the same. For example, "I've changed," "I wish someone would have shared this with me when I first started," "I have trouble sleeping now," "I get so angry now, I don't have any more patience," "I've had heart palpitations," "My family tells me that I'm not affectionate anymore," "This training and information needs to be given to management, to everyone, now!"

In my survey I asked, among other questions, "After being to this training, how would you rate the importance of self-care?" I provided a scale of one through five, with five representing "very important." With only about a 3 percent exception in the hundreds of surveys that I've collected, the participants circled five. The 3 percent circled three or four.

So many social workers and helping professionals, paid and volunteer, still aren't aware of this VT impact. Our agencies and systems have yet to take a comprehensive and meaningful appraisal of this clear and unquestionably profound effect on their helping professionals.

All social workers and other helping professionals *can do something about VT* and should not wait for their respective agencies to realize the very critical issue of self-care. We can take practical, meaningful steps now to mitigate the potentially damaging effects of VT on our physical, professional, and personal lives. At the end of this chapter is a list of reported physical and mental health concerns associated with VT.

We can educate ourselves about VT and take steps to develop a personalized self-care strategy as part of the work itself. Self-care needs to and can be built into the very job itself.

Some suggestions that I provide in my VT trainings:

1) Increase the time that you spend with people and activities that infuse your life with meaning: friends, children, partner, hobbies, interests, volunteering, music, etc.

2) Create an informal or formal process with a colleague, buddy, or group. Share with a loved one "above the chin" but process the feelings generated from your traumatized client "below the chin."

3) Maintain positive human connections.

4) Incorporate self-reflection tools, such as journaling, processing with a colleague, or spending time alone to silently reflect. This will help you monitor your VT level and stay grounded in your original core beliefs.

5) Have diversified roles where you don't carry the weight of a trauma worker, where you can relinquish control and responsibility, where you can be playful and frivolous, laugh out loud, and just have fun.

Above all, self-care must become a *daily* practice, a necessary part of the important and challenging work that we find so rewarding. This can't be just a sidebar that we record on some to-do list and always relegate to some lesser importance so that we never end up doing it. It must be done daily if we are ever going to have a healthy, productive, effective and affective, consistently empathic, strength-based, and sustainable workforce of social workers and other helping professionals.

To paraphrase a quote that truly captures my training's closing remarks: We all have a moral imperative to our loved ones, our clients, our professions, and, most importantly, to ourselves to do this work in a way that does not damage the self.

Social Workers Health Crisis

Agitation, inability to relax

- Apathy
- Anger toward perpetrators or causal events
- Anxiety

- Anxious or racing thoughts
- Back pain
- Becoming cynical
- Becoming fearful and or pessimistic and dreading coming to work
- Becoming miserable
- Becoming jaded
- Behavior and judgment impaired
- Feelings that you are incompetent
- Blurred vision due to stress
- Body pains
- Breast cancer (due to chronic stress)
- Burnout
- Chest pain
- Compromised cognitive ability
- Cognitive difficulties with memory and perception
- Constant worrying
- Compromised psychological needs, such as trust, safety, esteem, control, intimacy, etc.
- Compulsive eating
- Chemical dependency
- Depression and PTSD
- Despair and loss of hope
- Diabetes
- Developing a feeling and belief of incompetence
- Digestive problems
- Diminishing objectivity when working with families
- Disruption of professional and personal relationships
- Dizziness

- Eating too much or too little
- Emotionally drained
- Emotional intensity increases
- Emotional stress
- Excessive stiffness in the shoulders
- Exhaustion
- Fatigue
- Feeling overwhelmed
- Gastrointestinal aliment due to stress (heartburn, acid reflux, GERD, ulcers)
- Grief and loss
- Hair loss
- Headaches
- Heart attack
- High blood pressure
- Irregular menstrual cycles
- Loss of self-worth and emotional modulation
- Loss of hope and meaning, existential despair
- Malaise
- Memory problems
- Miscarriages
- Moodiness
- More irritable
- Nausea
- Neck pain
- Nervous habits (nail biting, pacing)
- Nightmares
- Numerous car accidents resulting from excess anxiety and distress

- Panic attacks
- Paranoia
- Personal relationships decrease
- Physical nervous system arousal affecting nutrition, exercise, and sleep
- Preterm labor
- Rapid heartbeat
- Sciatica in right leg
- Seeing only the negative stress
- Self-medicating
- Sense of loneliness or isolation
- Sleeping too much or too little
- Sleepless nights, especially before returning to work on Monday
- Stomachaches
- Stomach issues/hiatal hernia
- Stress on the heart
- Stroke
- Tingling sensations
- Tenosynovitis (inflammation of the lining of the sheath that surrounds a tendon)
- Using alcohol and cigarettes to relax
- Weight loss or gain
- Withdrawal from social activity
- Work performance decreases
- **Death****

**The deaths by heat attack of a number of social workers have been directly attributed to their jobs.

The Bureaucratic Iron Curtain

I had been working for DCFS for about six years. I was working as a lead dependency investigator (DI). It was my third job title at that point. As a DI, my job was to conduct extensive investigations into allegations that we filed against parents regarding any alleged maltreatment, abuse, or neglect of children.

My only concern with my new job function was to make my boss and her boss happy. It became crystal clear very quickly that the way to excel in this new position was to "give the teacher what she wanted." If I could make Mother Teresa look guilty, and I could—I had the skill set and I was good at it—I would be showered with praise and endless recognition. The actual truth had little to nothing to do with my job.

My job was to ensure that every single allegation in our petition, regardless of whether or not it was accurate, fair, or even true, was sustained. *Sustained* is legal jargon for "ordered true, or true enough for our court." The burden of proof with our court came from the state Welfare and Institution Codes (WIC), the laws that governed us. These codes required a "preponderance of evidence." Picture the scale used to symbolize our legal system, the one held by a blindfolded Lady Justice, signifying that justice is blind. Take that scale and make sure both sides are equal. Now find maybe one or two feathers and place them on one side of the scale, tipping the scale just slightly. This would indicate that the burden to provide a "preponderance of evidence" that a stated fact is true has been met. That is a practical analogy to the meaning of that phrase.

I noticed that CSWs seem to come and go so quickly. It reminded me of something a colleague and friend told me on one of my first days on the job. She said, "I am so personally happy to see you, but professionally I feel so sorry for you." At the time, I didn't quite understand what she meant. I found her words puzzling and slightly troubling, but I quickly dismissed them as her having a bad day. I later realized just how prophetic her words really were.

I was now forming some good working relationships with workers and supervisors based on mutual respect. The rate of attrition continued to be dramatic. CSWs seemed to be dropping like flies, leaving many of us half-kiddingly saying that the life expectancy of a CSW was the same as that of a common housefly.

As I started to pay more attention to my colleagues, what I saw and heard began to deeply disturb me. Clearly, something about the job was having a profound and devastating effect on CSWs.

I started to pull from all my educational experience and realize that it was time to hit the books again. For those of us with a master's degree (mine is in Marriage, Family, and Child Counseling), once we earn it, we quite humbly come to realize that our degrees teach us that we have so much more to learn.

I had been out of school for some time, having finished my graduate studies several years earlier. I researched everything I could about CSW burnout and found some great studies. One in particular was "Stressors in Child Welfare Practice" by Phillip Howe and Corinne McDonald. Howe was the assistant director and McDonald was the human resource manager for the Children's Aid Society of Toronto (CAST). This was a comprehensive landmark study that later provided me with just the springboard I needed to develop my own model. I was turned on to this study because McDonald was by then a DCFS manager I had worked with on various special projects. I also got to know Howe from corresponding with him via e-mail. He was very gracious and supportive and very generous with his knowledge and experience. For that, I'll be eternally grateful.

In the original 2001 study, which investigated the stressors behind social-worker burnout, Howe found that between 46 and 90 percent of child-welfare practitioners turn over in two years, the result of constant exposure to traumatized families and children and threats or assaults on their person. This leaves CSWs exhibiting PTSD-like symptoms.

As a way of addressing and mitigating the traumatic stress that Howe saw with his social-worker colleagues, he developed an innovative peer-support model. He would mobilize what he called a peer-support team (PST) composed of volunteer social workers who would support social workers who had recently experienced a critical incident. A "critical incident" included death, attempted suicide, illness or disease, threats, assaults, and injuries.

What was abundantly clear was that peer support was the single most powerful and important feature for any type of meaningful support for social workers, and social workers repeatedly took advantage of the service.

When one understands the nature of traumatic stress, one realizes the tremendous benefit and absolute necessity of social workers providing mindful, formalized, daily, and ongoing support to and for each other. Very simply put, when a social worker shares his or her emotional reaction with another social worker, several significant and therapeutic realities unfold.

First, when a CSW empathically listens to a colleague sharing his or her emotional response to an encounter with a traumatized client, the CSW validates this colleague. As the CSW does this, he or she encourages the colleague to fully process this emotional encounter (they're all emotional encounters to some degree or another, that's the point!). As the colleague processes his or her response, this helps to avoid an emotional buildup that, when left unattended, can and will wreak havoc on his or her emotional and psychological self.

Validation occurs almost instantaneously when it comes from peers. They have walked and are walking in our shoes. Peers are not burdened by this emotional processing. Quite the contrary, they have validated their own emotional encounters (which they all are, that's the point!).

I caution CSWs not to try this with spouses, partners, or intimates because they're not trained to hear it. The rule is to *share* the narrative with your intimates "above the chin," and *process* with CSW peers "below the chin."

Secondly, as the CSW listens to and encourages the colleague to process the emotional experience, the CSW is validated for his or her emotional encounters because he or she has also had a handful or more encounters with traumatized clients (they're all traumatized, that's the point!).

Thirdly, these two CSWs are building a professional bond and, simultaneously, establishing and strengthening a solid line of communication between each other. The burgeoning or reinforced bond provides the basis for a vital, readily accessible, almost daily VT support system, to help mitigate the potentially devastating effects of VT.

I took what I learned from Howe, my research, my graduate-level education, and my direct observations of my social-worker colleagues, and developed my peer-support team model.

I pitched my local office, and after several conversations with the powers that be and multiple informal and formal meetings, I got the green light. I was flying solo, so I was going to start by formally introducing my PST model to my colleagues and providing in-office support for any critical incidents in our office. I was so excited.

But at the eleventh hour, I got word to stop. I later found out that a union representative had learned of my intentions and told the office head that I had "no right encroaching on union territory and business." The rep thought that it was the union's business and jurisdiction to provide this type of support to CSWs. I still can't believe what this representative did. Despite my repeated efforts and impassioned pleas to go forward, it was clear that this union rep had seriously spooked my office head. My model was stillborn.

I'm not exactly sure how much time had gone by, but one day I received a call from a stranger named Charlene. She and her colleague, James, both worked as coordinators for our DCFS Clinical Licensure program and were very interested and passionate about addressing the VT of our CSWs.

We met and I shared the model that I had developed and told them the incredibly unbelievable story of how the union rep had derailed it. We all agreed to collaborate and develop my model into a peer-support program that had county- and agency-wide application. Like me, they clearly had seen too much hurt, pain, and devastation among our CSW colleagues, and were unalterably and passionately committed to doing something about it. It was exciting! As we established our game plan, we assigned different pieces of what we were developing to each other for later review. Later, we recruited two other colleagues, one of whom remained and became a very valuable and important partner. Her name was Eddie.

We spent the next eight years of our professional lives trying to implement PST as we simultaneously juggled our regular DCFS work and personal lives. Our collective efforts resulted in a very economically feasible, clinically solid, and undeniably evidenced-based program that was specifically and uniquely developed for our DCFS agency. We couldn't automatically obtain DCFS's buy-in and resources, but we eventually figured out a plan.

Our first effort looked very hopeful. Our then-director was

very gracious and granted us a face-to-face meeting. We pitched, and he understood right away the obvious need. His enthusiasm was wonderful, but he was also realistic and pragmatic. DCFS operates like a collection of little fiefdoms, so he had limited influence.

He said, "Look, I probably have a chance to do one to three things a year, that's it." Still, he gave us the thumbs-up. He congratulated and thanked us for our hard work and dedication to helping our colleagues. He said that he was going to instruct his executive team to make PST happen. Wow! *Hey, this is actually going to happen,* we thought, perhaps naively.

We would spend the rest of this director's tenure attending meeting after meeting and answering e-mail after e-mail after e-mail with the other executive committee members. We did our best to answer every question and address every concern, yet the e-mails kept coming, the concerns repeating themselves but with different wording.

The years passed. Our frustration and fatigue grew, but we had known that it wasn't going to be easy. We were essentially proposing an absolute change for DCFS, a culture with an infamous history of fighting hard to maintain the status quo at all costs, even when the alternative is clearly beneficial. We were attempting to do something that, to the best of our knowledge, had never been done or proposed in a child-welfare agency, and to do so in one that was quite possibly the largest public child protection agency on the planet. We were trying to demonstrate that VT is a reality that we could not ignore, that it was our duty to change the very nature and function of our CSW jobs to include this PST model to mitigate VT.

Sometimes it seemed like we were getting close, only to melt into disappointment after disappointment. It became clear that the executive committee was stonewalling us. In Congress, it's called "dying in committee." To paraphrase something I once heard, politics is the art of stalling long enough until people either get too tired to move on or eventually just forget. That was happening here.

The director left, much time passed, and we still had our regular DCFS work. We got new directors, which is not uncommon if you stick around long enough.

One day, after our model had lain dormant for some time, I received a call from someone who wanted me to come to a manager's office and talk about PST. That manager was the one who had first introduced me to Phillip Howe and was now our director. Talk about a small world. The manager was interested in PST, but before rallying Charlene, James, and Eddie, I wanted to make sure that this apparent show of interest was real. The manager told me, in no uncertain terms, that it was. So I called the team, and after much discussion and soul-searching, remembering just how emotionally, physically, and spiritually taxing the first go-around was, we unanimously decided to give it another try.

So, once again, we attended meeting after meeting, answered e-mail after e-mail, and addressed concern after concern. But this time it seemed even more likely to happen. This was the second director who recognized and understood the very obvious need and potential benefit that could come from PST. She knew of the years and years of work that went into PSTs development. She had known me from when I had first conceptualized PST and developed it into an actual model. She had also known the rest of our team for years and had no doubt about our commitment, skill, and collective credentials. It had to happen now, right?

So we attended more meetings and answered more e-mails and waited and waited and waited. By now, we had a comprehensive booklet that contained every detail about PST (thanks to Eddie, who did much of our editing). We answered questions and addressed concerns. Then, in one meeting with the executive committee, one committee member said something that I'll never forget.

"Do we even need it?"

That ignorant and ridiculous statement spoke volumes about how and why PST would possibly never be.

Another oft-repeated concern was that CSWs might share feelings and make statements that did not reflect well on their supervisors, colleagues, or the department. Or maybe a CSW's issues would somehow unnecessarily expose DCFS to some form of liability.

We had anticipated all these concerns and had already built safeguards for these and many other potential issues. These contingencies were clearly and methodically laid out in our PST booklet. We did our very best to assuage these and all other voiced, e-mailed, implied, or intimated concerns, over and over and over.

Once again, it was a case of waiting or stalling until people just got too tired or simply forgot. This second director eventually left. When she did, we never tried again.

At least eight years of our professional lives had now elapsed. We maintained our day jobs and our personal lives and went on.

PST never made it past the DCFS bureaucratic iron curtain. Even after two consecutive directors (one male, the other female), who were seemingly the most influential and powerful individuals in our culture, ordered it to happen, and even after our agency identified a clear and unimpeachable need, the bureaucratic iron curtain fell on this brief passage of our professional lives.

I'm probably just stubborn by nature, but I haven't given up on PST. The desperate need hasn't changed and isn't going to anytime soon. VT is our asbestos in the walls. Its potentially devastating effects on our workforce will discreetly, slowly, and certainly continue to ravage our CSWs. Mounting research and our own collective eyes and ears have already provided all the evidence we need—even for a standard as high as "beyond a reasonable doubt."

The potential benefit from PST, or some peer-support model, is undeniable. Merely offering an occasional class on compassion fatigue, which is great information for beginning to build an understanding of our traumatic stress, falls seriously short of what's needed. Offering a class even on VT is profoundly inadequate and misses the target by miles, and that becomes clear once one truly understands what VT is and how it manifests itself in the lives of CSWs.

We don't need to do any more research, we certainly don't need any more committee work, and God knows we don't need any more e-mails.

What we need is to find a way to bring down our bureaucratic iron curtain. We need to find the courage and determination to act, not on supposition or conjecture or theory but on what we're collectively seeing and hearing and what we have endured as CSWs. We all need to grab that cord and pull.

How to Begin Fixing the System

There are no easy answers or quick fixes. We're not offering a panacea. Many of the systemic deficiencies and flawed, deleterious practices cited in this book have had decades or longer to germinate and grow into the very fabric of our DCFS culture. Our bureaucratic system is huge, our infrastructure massive, our personnel numbers in the thousands, and our agency spread over a massive geographical area. Addressing the issues chronicled in this book is, at best, multilayered, complex, and daunting. But the need to address them is increasingly urgent and absolutely paramount.

We make the following suggestions as starting points, not as a final destination. Our overarching goal is to open a constructive discourse on how all concerned stakeholders, CSWs, administration and management staff, case families, and community members can mobilize and come together not as adversaries but as citizens mutually concerned for the welfare of our communities' at-risk children and their families. *The singular goal is to make DCFS better.*

That entails building on the existing strengths, progress, and accomplishments of DCFS so that we can continue to provide the best possible community service to our case families, helping protect children and preventing abuse and neglect by supporting families in confronting their child's at-risk issues through a service built on respect, cultural awareness, factual truths, and empowerment.

Here, then, are our suggestions:

On Writing and Submitting Court Reports

Our longstanding, seriously flawed, and pernicious court report writing and submission practices have essentially gone unchecked and unchallenged, absolutely free from any meaningful review. It will not be easy to substantively change. There will no doubt be much resistance. Our bureaucracy, as with most, fights to maintain the status quo at all costs. However, the stakes are too high and our responsibility to each other and, most importantly, to our case families is too great to allow the daunting nature and challenge of the task to supplant the incredible need to act now. We strongly suggest that a new policy be implemented.

I. If a supervisor and/or an administrator (either an ARA or RA) substantively alters and/or amends a court report in a way that disagrees with the CSW's findings, that supervisor and/or administrator must be **required** to sign the report and be prepared to represent said report in court should the court wish to question the report's **actual** author. The supervisor and/ or administrator also will be **required** to tell the family that he/she is the author and that he/she and not the CSW is making the recommendations as a representative of the department.

Regarding court reports, a supervisor and/or administrator may do only the following:

A. Check for and correct grammatical errors

B. Ensure the report meets all court requirements

C. Ensure the report is completed in a timely matter

D. Ensure the sources are verifiable

E. Ensure the recommendations are consistent with the facts

F. Ensure compliance with this policy

II. A supervisor and/or an ARA/RA will no longer order a CSW to make recommendations on a court report that disagree with the CSW's findings, as long as those findings are the product of the CSW's direct observations and/or the direct observations of other support-service providers and helping professionals working directly with the family that is the subject of the report.

III. No DCFS personnel, at any level, shall be allowed to include information in a report or have any influence—including and especially in the recommendation section—unless that person has met the family that is the subject and focus of the court report and has given the family an opportunity to discuss its concerns and share its points of view with the report's true author.

IV. CSWs cannot be penalized, harassed, disciplined, or retaliated against because they chose not to sign a report or represent a report in court that contains findings and/or recommendations that disagree with the CSW's findings, as long as those findings are the product of the CSW's direct observations and/or the direct observations of other support-service providers and helping professionals working directly with the family that is the subject of the report.

Our recommended policy, most importantly, will demand that all court reports be written with a higher degree of integrity, accuracy, and reliability and be based on the facts that the CSW has observed in working directly with the family and with taking time to experience and develop a working and informed relationship with the family. Therefore, there will be no more reports ghostwritten by anyone insulated from responsibility and accountability and who has never met the case family. As a result, courts will not have to guess at the truth and, if necessary, force the CSW to contradict the report's findings.

This policy, which may appear provocative and outrageous to some, would demand a bold new commitment to act with integrity and courage. This policy would challenge DCFS to rethink and redefine the CSW's role in managing a caseload.

Obviously, we need supervisors to provide guidance, mentoring, and oversight to their CSW subordinates. This definitely includes court reports and training new CSWs. These neophytes are just starting out and need close monitoring by their supervisor to maximize their growth and development.

Fortunately, DCFS has supervisors and administrators who try very hard to use the above criteria when reviewing and approving the court reports. When they do, the system works as it was intended. When the facts and matching recommendations in these court reports are made this way, the court is able to make an informed decision, render a proper legal finding, and make orders accordingly. This is the system working.

However, many DCFS supervisors and administrators will often marginalize and dismiss out of hand a CSW's findings and recommendations and instead substitute someone else's subjective version of the family's status, which leads to another set of recommendations. When this occurs, our system does not work. The result is at best tragic and at worst catastrophic for our CSWs, their supervisors, and, most critically, our case families. THIS MUST STOP!

Our families deserve better, and our CSWs, supervisors, and administrators are waiting to be unshackled, to be able to speak freely and report the truth without retaliation and retribution, maybe even with the department's support and gratitude.

Find Our Moral Compass

For our agency to truly benefit from any potentially positive system changes and organizational growth, we must first address the need for a clearly defined and institutionally embraced moral compass. This compass's guiding principles place the best interest and welfare of our case families first, demand the fair and considerate treatment of each other, permeate every policy and protocol, and become the precursor for every decision and action in performing our respective jobs.

In short, this moral compass should be the foundation of our collective standard of conduct. Absent this, we'll continue to ask the following sobering questions over and over:

* *Why is a supervisor able to tell a CSW, "Well, just lie—after all, that's what families do," and this supervisor is promoted to ARA?*

* *Why can supervisors and/or administrators compel a CSW to walk into open court and promise to tell the truth, the whole truth, and nothing but the truth—and then lie?*

* *Why can supervisors and/or administrators insist that their subordinates represent falsehoods under the rationale of "we speak with one voice"?*

* *When did "we speak with one voice" stop requiring a morally correct decision grounded in truth?*

* *Why can a group of high-ranking managers force a lower-ranking administrator to harshly discipline a CSW or other staff for something when there is no evidence to support it? Where is due process?*

* *Why can ARAs get away with telling supervisors that their reports' numbers and statements cannot make them look bad?*

* *How can an RA be allowed to tell a CSW that, as retaliation for the CSW's refusal to lie on a court report, she's under investigation by Internal Affairs when she's not?*

* *Why can an ARA earn promotion to RA after demoting a probationary supervisor for standing up for the safety and welfare of two boys who eventually were taken out of the country?*

The challenges and complexities, which we manage day in and day out, make social work in child welfare among the toughest and most demanding jobs in our society. Therefore, having and acting in compete adherence to a moral compass is critically important, necessary, and urgent.

We know that finger-pointing will quickly start and we may be held accountable, rightly or wrongly, and that the vast majority of us will have to face the harshest and must punishing critic of all: ourselves. Our vicarious traumatization almost guarantees that.

If we can institutionally establish and genuinely promote a moral compass for our actions and the decisions that are made on all levels, we will be better prepared emotionally and psychologically to endure the external and internal pressures that will ensue when tragedies occur. We will also be better able to handle the pressures that exist in the demanding and complex day-to-day operations of our respective jobs.

How does an agency like ours create a lasting and effective moral compass? How do we make it concrete and viable in our day-to-day work? We need our leaders to come forward. That includes our board of supervisors, our director, our department deputies, our regional administrators, our assistant regional administrators, and our supervisors. We need our leaders to institute a *code of ethics and standard of practice that makes any onerous, destructive, anti-family, and anti-welfare practice impossible.*

Our Recommended Code of Ethics and Standards of Practice

* *That the best interest of our case families **is tantamount** to the best interest of our agency, and that the best interest of our case families is never to be relegated or subordinated to any agency or individual.*

* *That while understanding and interpreting facts can and will be for a myriad of reasons subject to debate and constructive and collaborative discourse, the facts **are not.***

* *That our department within DCFS is committed to truth and integrity in all our decisions and actions.*

* *That no DCFS staff shall ever be disciplined and/or mistreated for disclosing or acting on the facts that they have personally observed and experienced, or that have been reported by verifiable, approved, and accepted agency or community sources.*

* *That the directive "we speak with one voice" must always, without exception, ensure the moral correctness and factual accuracy of our decisions, and our individual and organizational responsibility to state and act on the truth.*

Let Us Take Care of Ourselves

We have an alarmingly long-overdue need to institutionalize self-care. We know with absolute certainty that we will experience vicarious traumatization. We know with absolute certainty that our VT will have a profound effect on us professionally and personally. We have a growing mountain of research and anecdotal evidence of VT's impact on our lives. We know that VT is our asbestos in the walls as we earnestly work to help our traumatized families. We know that it directly affects not just how we do our jobs, but our very natures, our core beliefs about others, our worldviews, and ourselves.

This isn't an eight-hundred-pound-gorilla-in-the-room scenario. It's an entire jungle of eight-hundred-pound gorillas screaming at the top of their lungs. Why hasn't DCFS meaningfully addressed this obvious area of concern? We are the greatest, most indisputable evidence of this. Just talk to any CSW, supervisor, or administrator (especially those who came up through the ranks) about how his or her work in child welfare has affected his or her life, if it has essentially changed who he or she is, and if it has negatively affected his or her family life. All the needed evidence is there.

We want to encourage the effective use of RAD:

R—Recognition of the issue

A—Acceptance of the issue

D—Doing something about it now!

We strongly recommend a peer-support team (PST) program like the one shared in the chapter "The Bureaucratic Iron Curtain." This program has the backing of years of research; its architects have a combined sixty-plus years of direct experience working in or being closely affiliated with DCFS. This program is comprehensive and has taken into account almost every conceivable consideration to make sure that it's compatible with our agency's structure and culture.

PST had the backing and support of not one but two DCFS directors. This program is specifically designed to help mitigate the pernicious affects of VT, and it does so in an economically feasible way. It has been designed to work within our current system framework. Its design is also flexible and can adjust to the realities out there. It's not perfect, but knowing what CSWs absolutely know and live with, how can we afford to let perfect be the enemy of good?

We don't need more endless committee discussions; we need to do something. We need to quickly focus our collective energy, experience, knowledge of the issue, talents, skills, and available resources to *do something now!* Viable and smart initiatives were brought forth in July of 2009 (see "Stories of Prevention in Los Angeles County: DCFS and Community Agencies Join Hands to Support Families and Children" from the Prevention Initiative Demonstration Project), but unfortunately, many of the initiatives appear to have fallen by the wayside and have not been incorporated into the policies and practices of DCFS.

We should have started taking care of our own a long time ago. Our CSWs and our support, supervisory, and managerial staff can and should be a happier, healthier, more productive, more efficient, and more sustainable body of child-welfare practitioners. We can and must provide the best possible to the case families that we are entrusted to serve to the very best of our collective abilities.

How CSWs Can Help Themselves

We are all significantly impacted when we empathically engage our traumatized clients and families. Using the below tips will go a long way to help mitigate this impact.

Question Everything

CSWs should not believe everything they hear from the caregiver, the foster family agency (FFA) caseworker, or the parents. Best practices should have a social worker be obliging, professional, and courteous to the information-giver. However, the next step is to verify that information. When a mother states, for example, that she is enrolled in a drug rehabilitation program, the CSW's duty is to call the mother's program and confirm this, or, better still, to speak with the mother's caseworker or counselor to check her progress in the program. When calling the drug program, the CSW might learn the mother is not enrolled. The purpose of the call is to verify the information. It is not, as some social workers believe, to play the *"Gotcha!"* game, where one strives to prove to everybody what a liar the parent is. This is a no-no. Ask the professional to author a letter on the mother's progress. At the very least, get a statement from the caseworker or counselor that can be incorporated into the court report. If the professional refuses, respectfully explain that he or she may be subpoenaed to appear in court to present the information. (Professionals can be subpoenaed in certain cases if their testimony is needed, so never say, "If you write a letter, you won't be asked into court.")

It is imperative that social workers observe the interactions between child and parents at regular intervals. Too many social workers rely on information supplied by third parties without checking things for themselves. Here are two examples:

1) I had a case involving a foster parent who stated that the two children under the age of five in her care were terrified of their mother. "When she calls them on the phone, they run and hide beneath tables," she said. The foster parent, who monitored the visits between the mother and the children, maintained that the children did not want to see their mother. The therapist (the kids were in play therapy), who had never met the mother, concurred with the foster mother that the children should not be forced to see their mother. When I told the foster parent the court had ordered further reunification services for the mother and that the visitations would continue, she rolled her eyes and shook her head.

I decided to monitor one of the visits myself. It was unforgettable. I picked up the children from their foster home and transported them to the mother. What I observed gave me a lump in my throat. The children were not terrified of their mother. It was the exact opposite. The children ran to their mother, screaming, "Mommy! Mommy!" They jumped into her lap. They hugged her. They held on to her for dear life. I observed that the affection was mutual. The mother hugged her children, smiled at them, and touched them often. She was good with them. When it was time for the visit to end, the children cried that they wanted their mommy. It was like a scene out of a movie in which I try to pry away their little fingers from around their mommy. I quickly let go of that idea. I extended the visit.

I disclosed to the foster parent what I had observed and told her I'd be looking for a new monitor during the times I wasn't available myself. The foster parent said that when the children came home from a visit, they misbehaved terribly and were hard to control. I explained that the children were young and could not articulate their feelings, so they acted out. My guess was that they didn't want to leave their mother and were reacting to the separation.

I monitored several more visits that confirmed my original observations. My next court report documented it all.

2) The other example involved an African-American single father. The foster parent made her intentions known early on that she'd like to adopt, and the FFA caseworker wrote letters to the social worker saying that although the father was a nice man, he hadn't taken care of his one-year-old daughter on any of the visits they monitored. He didn't change her diapers, he didn't feed her, he didn't keep her safe, and he didn't engage her. The social worker, who hadn't observed any of the visits himself, recommended that the father's parental rights be terminated.

When another witness to the visitations made it known that what was previously reported was inaccurate, that not only did the father know how to take care of his child but that the father and daughter were bonded, the case changed.

It is a social worker's obligation to find the facts. Court officers need the most accurate information on cases so they can make the best possible decision for a child.

Save Good Contacts

Good contacts, unfortunately, can be rare, so when a CSW finds a program or service that works, save it. Keep a file of sure-thing referrals in the desk or on the computer. It will make your job much easier. Unfortunately, budgets are cut and many programs fall by the wayside, so the list will always be a work in progress. Therefore, make sure to keep it current.

Don't be Too Quick to Label a Case a Failure

Two examples:

1) When I met Yolanda (all names have been changed to protect confidentiality), she was thirty-five and mother to six-

year-old Wesley and four-year-old Rashard. Both children had been diagnosed with attention deficit hyperactivity disorder (ADHD). Yolanda had a long history of methamphetamine addiction. As a result, her teeth had fallen out and she had lost custody of her children. She had prostituted herself for drugs, and her situation appeared bleak. The father's whereabouts were unknown. During the time I worked with Yolanda, she had graduated from an inpatient drug program but later relapsed. Her children had been in a foster home for eight months. I lost contact with Yolanda after a lateral job move took me off her case.

Twelve years later, as I walked across a parking lot, I heard my name being called. I turned around, and walking toward me was a very familiar-looking woman: Yolanda. She told me she had eventually freed herself from drug addiction and had regained custody of her boys. She smiled a beautiful smile. She explained that a dentist had helped her with new teeth. Yolanda told me that she never forgot what I had told her: that I had confidence that she could learn to live without drugs.

She said she remembered how I came to her drug rehab graduation and brought her flowers. She stated nobody had ever given her flowers before. Then a tall young man came up to Yolanda and stood beside her. It was a teenaged Rashard. She put her arm around him and as she reintroduced him to me and I shook his hand, my eyes teared up. We spoke for a while. I wished them both well, and we parted ways.

2) Charles was a four-year old boy who had been placed in twelve different foster homes. His foster parents would call and request his removal, citing behavioral issues like banging his head against the walls, throwing things, and refusing to eat with utensils. Further, the foster parents maintained that the child merely grunted and did not know how to speak. "He's just too much to handle," they'd state. "I need you to remove him—now."

I remember one time I picked up Charles from a former foster home to take him to his new home. On the way, I thought it would be a great idea to get him a chocolate shake, to possibly get his mind off things and make him happy. It always worked with my own children. I went through a drive-through with Charles strapped into his car seat in my back seat. I spoke in a happy tone to him. I handed Charles the shake, looked forward, and started driving.

The next thing I knew, Charles threw that chocolate shake at my head.

We arrived at Charles's new foster home, his twelfth. I'm sure I was quite the sight when the foster mother opened the door and found me standing at her doorstep with chocolate shake dripping from my hair, Charles's little hand in mine. Charles stood there with furrowed brow, grunting and hissing at her.

"Oh my!" she exclaimed. "Is he," she paused. "Is he a *good* boy?" she asked nervously.

"Oh, he's fine," I lied to her, and off he went into her home.

During this time, I had been writing to Charles's incarcerated father (Charles's mother had abandoned him). His letters back to me were baffling. He stated that it didn't sound like I was describing his son. Nevertheless, the father indicated to me he would soon be released from prison. He asked to see his son as soon as could possibly be arranged.

We scheduled a visitation for him to see Charles. When that day arrived, I remember taking Charles into the room where his father was seated and waiting for us to arrive. Charles walked into the room, did a double take when he saw his father, and then said very clearly, "Hey. Where's Mom?"

I almost fainted. "You *speak*?" I said to Charles, incredulously. I just shook my head. It had been eight months since Charles had come to the attention of DCFS.

From that day forward, Charles resembled any other four-year-old boy. He used words to communicate. He ate with utensils. He no longer hit his head against walls.

Charles's father also got his act together and did everything he needed to regain custody of his son. Father and son were reunited six months later. And six months after that, their case was closed.

Document Everything

Find an organizing system that works for you. When taking or making phone calls, jot down the date, summarize what's being said, and keep detailed notes on all pertinent points.

A common question new social workers ask is, "Should I let parents see what I'm writing when I'm interviewing them?" The answer: Yes, and there's a way to make this work. Say to the parent something along the lines of, "Do you mind if I take notes? I want to make sure I get down everything you're saying." Moreover, keep your pad of paper down in plain sight, and when you're finished, read back to the parent what you heard him or her say to ensure your notes are accurate.

Occasionally, I find somebody who would prefer me not to jot things down or find myself in a situation where taking notes doesn't work with the situation (for example, spending time with a teenaged client and gauging his or her point of view). In these instances, a CSW should wait until he or she is alone to pull out paper and a writing utensil and start documenting. I pull into the parking lot of a local twenty-four-hour restaurant to write my notes shortly after leaving an interview.

There's another reason to document everything. It's called Cover Your Ass. One of the first things I learned while working for DCFS was to CYA. When something goes wrong, the DCFS culture is to blame others and point fingers. Taking responsibility for one's actions isn't common. So when the finger comes pointing, have documentation to confirm.

Never Say Anything Negative about a Parent in Front of a Child

Despite parental abuse or neglect, many children speak of their parents in glowing terms. Yes, something needs to change to lessen or eliminate the behavior that brought the parents to DCFS's attention in the first place, but this doesn't mean that the children don't love their parents anymore. A social worker must remember this and understand how strong the parent–child bond is. Many a social worker has made some derogatory remark regarding a mother or father in the child's presence and then discovered that the child–social worker bond was fatally wounded.

Don't Ask Somebody to Do Something You Wouldn't Do

We've heard social workers tell their teenaged case children that they will be switching schools again as if it's no big deal. Or these social workers will not return phone calls to parents or will exclude parents who retain their full rights from important information regarding their children. Or they require parents to travel six hours round-trip on a bus to visit their children. Or they explain to parents that they may only see their children once per week because of the social worker or foster parent's schedule. CSWs should try to walk in another's shoes and ask how it would feel if somebody required the same of them. Before asking something of somebody, pause and then think, *Would this be okay for me, too?*

Take Your Teen Clients for a Ride

Some of the best conversations I've had with teens have taken place while driving them in the car. They tend to open up and talk when CSWs aren't staring at them.

Know What Works

I find humor in things, and I tend to be quick-witted. It helps to have a sense of humor in this business. What also works for me is participating in advanced training. How to properly conduct a sexual abuse interview, how to excel as a supervisor, becoming culturally competent and undoing racism: all that training is out there. But CSWs have to seek it out. It won't come to them. With regards to undoing racism, sadly, racial discrimination against African American children and their families remains ever present in child welfare.

Along the lines of what works, know what doesn't. Melvy Murguia of Quantum Coaching, who provided me management training while I was with CASA (Court Appointed Special Advocates), helped me, among other things, to reframe my "failures" as behaviors that didn't work. What works and what doesn't is a very useful concept to utilize in both the professional and personal arenas.

Prepare for the Unexpected

Around 1993, I worked as a caseworker at a runaway shelter for children aged twelve to seventeen who were involved in prostitution and/or pornography. An acid substance that had been splashed into her eyes before she was raped had tragically blinded a fourteen-year-old client. I drove her to an eye doctor in the pouring rain to see if any part of her vision could be salvaged.

We were driving on the freeway with the windshield wipers working at full speed. The next thing I knew, a gust of wind blew my wipers off my car! I couldn't believe it. I was about to react by screaming, but I couldn't because I had a blind fourteen-year-old child sitting next to me and I didn't want to alarm her.

Still, I let out a yelp, and she asked me what the matter was. "It's nothing, honey," I lied while quivering. My heart was beating loudly and quickly. I couldn't see. I put on the right blinkers and my hazard lights and somehow made my way to the side. We remained there until the rain subsided then ventured onward.

Moral of the story: make sure to keep your car in working order and have everything checked before transporting children. I've had my windshield wipers replaced whenever needed ever since. CSWs with no sense of direction should consider investing in a navigation system.

Social workers sometimes work into the night or when it's dark outside. I remember visiting a home where a mother resided with her four daughters far from any signs of civilization. When it came time for me to leave, the mother walked me to the door and said in broken English with a genuinely scared look on her face, "Please look out for the snakes with the shakers on their tails!"

YIKES! I thought. It was pitch black and all I knew was that my car was parked over yonder with a sea of dirt and brush between safety and me. The next day, I bought one of those little flashlights sold at gas stations and kept it on me during future evening home visits.

Social workers sometimes work long hours visiting their clients. To keep from passing out from hunger, keep a stash of healthy survival foods in the car.

Know Your Biases

Everybody has biases. Unfortunately, DCFS does not match cases to social workers. Instead, cases are assigned randomly. So it's common, for example, for a social worker who cannot stand promiscuous teenaged females to be given a case with a promiscuous teenaged female. It doesn't take much to deduce that the youth might not get the services and treatment she deserves and needs. Or a social worker who thinks all children should be adopted might turn in a court report that unjustly paints a scathing picture of the parents.

Ethically, if a CSW cannot do a case justice because of bias, it is best to talk to the supervisor and ask to trade a case to a coworker with whom there won't be a conflict. Unchecked biases run rampant in the DCFS system, with social workers and higher-ups unintentionally harming the very population they swore to serve.

Also, know that this field tends to attract people with past hurts. It seems like many—from child-welfare workers to bailiffs to security guards to attorneys to hearing officers to therapists and so on—working in the field have a story to tell. I don't think it's coincidental that people are drawn to this line of work. Most have resolved their issues and are able to pull empathy from their experiences and impart it upon others. They become skilled at empowering those struggling souls.

Then there are the "walking wounded": professionals who are easily triggered and react to persons and situations quite negatively and unreasonably. They haven't successfully worked out their own situations and stressors, so their decision making is suspect and their ability to effect change is minimal at best.

Some Others:

* Form a processing group or find a partner and talk with them daily. This will help avoid the building-up of emotions that we will generate as we continue to empathically engage our traumatized families.

* Keep a journal and write in it every day; it will help you feel and stay grounded. Practicing mindful, consistent, daily self-care will not only help maintain better personal health, but also help weather our agency's crises and bureaucratic missteps.

* Call a loved one every day and don't talk about work.

* Feel good and complete based on the hours put in, *not* on the end result and *not* on the outcome of the clients' choices,

decisions, and behaviors. Then develop instant amnesia as soon as the workday ends.

* Keep infusing life with meaningful things such as hobbies, time with friends and family, and other creative and fun pursuits.

* Take walks, when possible, with a colleague.

* Join a gym or find a park, and use it during lunch breaks.

* Remember that you're not alone in what you're feeling.

A Final Warning

Ethos is defined as: "the distinguishing character, sentiment, moral nature, or guiding beliefs of a person, group, or institution." I don't know when, why, or how DCFS lost its ethos in its decision-making processes. But it did, and in a big way.

When an institution such as DCFS loses its ethos, it's at serious risk of having its institutional fears take over and run rampant. These fears include disapproval from a boss or a boss's boss, outside pressure or scrutiny, loss of personal advancement or the chance of it, and retaliation if we disagree and offer a dissenting voice to that part of our rigid and controlling culture that will not tolerate any opposition.

When our institutional fears supplant our moral principles and bury our ethos so deep that we can't find any trace of it, we simply and tragically lose our way. Many of the systemic deficiencies that we've talked about in this book; have personally experienced; or have been borne of tragic, enraging, and horrific stories of maltreatment from countless CSWs can be traced to the absence of a clear, definitive, and compelling ethos.

We believe that any meaningful discussion about how to address the systemic deficiencies that we speak of in this book needs to start with digging up the ethos of DCFS.

We desperately need to regain a stronghold on our ethos. What are the guiding principles that we at DCFS will always, without exception, apply in our policies, rules, procedures, protocols, decision-making processes, and, most importantly, our governances and guides on how to treat each other?

Without our ethos, we will continue to have, as we have had for far too long, such instances as CSWs being forced to sign off on reports that don't reflect their findings and what they know to be the truth. Instead, supervisors, ARAs, or RAs will react out of fear and insist on CSWs slanting (or worse) the report and making recommendations that conform to previous department positions or their personal subjective opinions because they don't want to appear inconsistent, or because a CSW isn't, in their subjective view, harsh enough toward the alleged offending party, and it'll come back "to bite them." The supervisor, ARA, or RA may also act out of fear of losing face with their boss, enduring possible community or political scrutiny, or experiencing the loss of advancement or a chance at it.

We will also continue to have numerous instances in which administrators and supervisors are told that they must discipline, often harshly, CSWs because of community or politically based scrutiny, which occurs for various reasons. The most notable reason, which is almost without exception sensationalized in the media, is the death of a child. Administrators, managers, and supervisors, long before actual, concrete fault can be determined, are routinely told to find somebody to take the fall. Administrators who are already trying and finding it harder and harder to hold on to their integrity come under intense distress as they again find themselves in this nightmare of cognitive dissonance and moral dilemmas.

Worse still, the entire DCFS culture knows that when "the shit hits the fan" and something goes wrong on a case, such as a profound tragedy like a child's death, regardless of what they did right and all the mitigating circumstances of their direct or indirect involvement as a CSW case worker, they will be thrown under the bus. What does it say about our agency when this is the understood and accepted reality of its workforce?

We will continue to lose CSWs who have been forced out on

the heels of threats, intimidation, or coercion by having to do something that they know is wrong, such as signing off on a report that they know to be untrue and potentially damaging to his or her case family. These CSWs become profoundly cynical and hopeless, apathetic and helpless, and they end up shutting down inside as a way to just get by and try to survive from paycheck to paycheck.

Without our ethos, we will also continue the inhumane practice of treating a CSW or supervisor who may be under review by Internal Affairs as a pariah. We will continue to ignore the profound emotional and psychological effect on the CSW and possibly his or her supervisor when IA comes knocking. We will continue to neglect providing them with timely, qualified, accessible, and ongoing support. We will continue to turn a seemingly indifferent eye to the effects of an IA review that leaves the CSW or supervisor traumatized and devastated, and that often causes the CSW or supervisor to take medical leave due to stress, shut down, or quit.

I call the group that shuts down "the walking dead." These are the CSWs and supervisors who feel so indelibly and emotionally scarred that they consciously or unconsciously go on autopilot, coming to work and just going through the motions. These walking dead constitute a sobering percentage of our CSW work-force.

Without our ethos, we at DCFS will continue to ignore the obvious, evidence-based effects that working with a traumatized population has on our CSWs and other supporting staff.

We will continue to abdicate our institutional responsibility to educate our neophyte CSWs about vicarious traumatization (VT) and its potentially devastating effects so that they can start their careers with the knowledge they need to practice daily self-care, remain healthy and thrive in their chosen field, and be able to do their jobs in a non-damaging way. This must be the case for not only the newbies but for all of our existing and seasoned CSW staff.

Without our ethos, we will continue to ignore our need and responsibility to thoughtfully reexamine the urgent and long-standing necessity of reconfiguring the CSW job. We must redesign the job to institutionalize and incorporate self-care to help mitigate VT. Our sobering historic and current attrition rates prove our need to address these issues so that we'll have a fighting chance of obtaining and maintaining a healthy, happy, thriving, and sustainable CSW workforce.

Finding and embracing our ethos will help us navigate our troubled system-deficient waters so we can prioritize the individual and collective welfare of our DCFS workforce and help prevent child abuse and neglect by providing our very best service and care to our case families.

One final warning involves the following. The Orange County Child Protective Services lost a 4.9-million-dollar lawsuit when social workers were found to have lied on a case and fabricated evidence to the court, and, further, for the county's failing to properly train employees about parents' constitutional rights. Orange County lost its appeal and the award is now ten million.

CPSIA information can be obtained at www.ICGtesting.com
Printed in the USA
LVOW06s0926240814

400611LV00003B/325/P